GW00913715

ASTROLOGY

ASTROLOGY

Katina

TREASURE PRESS

First published in 1981 by
Park Lane Press

This edition published in 1985 by
Treasure Press
59 Grosvenor Street
London W1

Text: © Katina 1981
Illustrations: © Gail Lewton 1981

Reprinted 1985

ISBN 1 85051 063 6

Printed in Hong Kong

CONTENTS

A brief history of astrology · 6

A BRIEF HISTORY OF ASTROLOGY

INTRODUCTION

> Had we never seen the stars, and the sun, and the heavens, none of the words which we have spoken about the Universe would ever have been uttered. But now the sight of day and night, and the months and revolutions of the years, have created number, and have given us a conception of Time; and the power of enquiring about the nature of the Universe; and from this source we have derived Philosophy, than which no greater good was or will be given by the gods to mortal Man.

Plato: the *Timaeus*

Plato's words remind us of the powerful effect that celestial phenomena have had on the development of man's reasoning powers ever since ancient times when our primitive ancestors started to trace connections between what goes on in the heavens and what happens on earth. Totally dependent as they were for survival on natural forces over which they had no control, they were constantly reminded that the most potent forces were located high above them in the sky.

Deeply implanted in all living creatures is the instinct for survival, and this would motivate men's efforts to come to terms with any forces superior to their own limited capabilities. Primitive man was unable to distinguish between the animate and inanimate phenomena of Nature; they would time their activities to coincide with natural forces which they thought of as actual beings.

We have no means of ascertaining exactly when primitive man first made deliberate and methodical use of the stars as calendar and compass. But we do have evidence that the people of prehistoric times must have done so. Before civilization reached western Europe, the inhabitants of Britain were among those making very practical use of their astronomical knowledge – witness Stonehenge, which was constructed on astronomical principles and was not only a site of religious rituals, but also an astronomical observatory. Indeed, according to some astronomers, it was also an astronomical computer that could be used to predict the positions of the sun, moon and eclipses, if not over an indefinite period, at least for some hundreds of years. In the Near East, which has been called the cradle of

According to astronomers G. S. Hawkins and Fred Hoyle, the megalithic sun-temple of Stonehenge was also a giant astronomical computer by which the times of solstices and solar and lunar eclipses could be predicted.

civilization, the people responsible for building the earliest civilizations organized them in accordance with their astronomical knowledge and their astrological beliefs. It must be borne in mind that astronomy and astrology were very closely interrelated in the minds of the people living in pre-Christian eras, and indeed right up to the seventeenth century AD, and that both were closely woven into early religions.

It is therefore no exaggeration to state that the practical application of astronomy – which, in essence, is what astrology is – played a very important part in the development of civilization. Its imprint is to be found on the history of medicine, of chemistry, it stimulated the imagination of those who gave us some of the greatest works of art, and it influenced the ideas of architects. And – to return to Plato once again – it steered the most profound thinkers among men into the realms of philosophy.

But, before dealing in brief with the history of astrology it would be as well to make clear to readers what its claims were – and what they are now.

Originally, the practice of astrology was based upon a belief that man's fate was governed by celestial deities – who ranked supreme over all other deities – and that he had no choice but to submit to the will of the gods. But today, no practitioner of astrology would postulate that 'the stars rule mankind' but rather that by the exercise of freewill man can bring his own impulses – indicated· by the pattern of his horoscope – under control, and thus deal that much better with any circumstances in which he finds himself.

THE ROLE OF ASTROLOGY IN EARLY CIVILIZATIONS

Astrology in Mesopotamia

The recorded history of astrology begins in Mesopotamia (now known as Iraq) when the first true civilization was founded there by the Sumerians. The Sumerian kingdom grew up in the delta between the lower reaches of the Tigris and Euphrates rivers but, during the course of its three-thousand-year history, it was to expand over the whole area of Mesopotamia and exercise a powerful influence on other civilizations in the Near and Middle East, and in the eastern Mediterranean.

The Sumerians were a highly intelligent and very inventive people, and had vast knowledge of astronomy and mathematics. The knowledge they imparted to the people who conquered (and obliterated) them was so advanced that in Mesopotamia astronomy and mathematics developed as true sciences in embryo. They were also the first people to devise a method of writing: the pictographs they cut into clay tablets were the first type of writing. But as they spoke a language totally unrelated to that of their conquerors, or of any other people in the Near East, translations had to be made, and these translations found their way all over Mesopotamia and beyond. A dictionary of Sumerian words and their Semitic equivalents was eventually compiled in the seventh century BC for the benefit of scribes, and it was unearthed by archaeologists in the nineteenth century. Since then historians have been made to realize that much of what they attributed to later Mesopotamian cultures had been derived from Sumerian sources.

In time, Babylon became the chief centre of Mesopotamian culture and that is why the Babylonians were often referred to as the source of astrological knowledge and astrological practice. For the vast amount of astronomical data that the Babylonians gathered together in the course of three thousand years was, of course, put to astrological use.

Throughout its history, Mesopotamian civilization was based on a religious pattern. From the monarch downwards, every member of society was involved in the service of a pantheon of deities. The most important were the gods of the sky, the atmosphere, and life-sustaining waters of the earth so vital to the Mesopotamians, who harnessed the flooding of the two great rivers by means of irrigation canals to provide an adequate supply of crops and ample pasturage. The other celestial gods were the Moon god (of much more importance to a people who based their activities primarily on a lunar calendar than the Sun god – though they also had a solar calendar) and a goddess identified with the planet Venus.

The priesthood invented a mythological account of the origin, formation and organization of the Universe, which can be translated in purely astronomical terms; from it we gather that the Babylonians – who had only the most crude instruments to aid them – were able, by purely visual observation, to predict accurately to within a fraction of a second the length of the lunar month, to distinguish and classify most of the constellations visible in the northern hemisphere, and to locate the equinoctial and solstitial periods of the year.

The Babylonians, in fact, mapped out the sky in great detail and paid particular attention to the rising and setting of certain stars. Their year dated from the time of the vernal equinox. Although they practised divination by other means and placed much faith in omens as a means of predicting events of importance to the welfare of the state and the well-being of the king, much of their observation and prediction relate to celestial phenomena, and especially the moon's appearance and phases. They were able to predict eclipses, but not with the degree of accuracy they showed in assessing the length of the lunar month. They were especially preoccupied with meteorological interpretations of celestial data – necessarily so as their economy was an agricultural one.

The casting of individual horoscopes was of no interest to them until their civilization was in its last stage; and by then they had been influenced by Greek ideas.

By that time – the fourth/third centuries BC – they had selected the twelve signs of the zodiac; by then, too, the planetary gods figured in their interpretation of the horoscopes of anyone who sought their services. But it would be a mistake to imagine that their horoscope interpretations were other than very cursory, giving very scant details of the characteristics and prospects of the people concerned.

We know very little about the Babylonian astrologers themselves; the most famous was Berosus, a Babylonian priest in the service of Marduk in Babylon. He lived in the third century BC and eventually settled on the island of Cos, where he supervised the teaching of astrology to students. The Hippocratic school of medicine was also located in Cos; we may assume that Berosus both contributed to and learned from what was taught there.

Another famous Babylonian stargazer was Kidinnu, who belongs to the fourth century BC. The only other one to be known by name was Naburiannu, who flourished around 500 BC. All were versed in astrological prediction.

The Babylonians were the first to build temple-observatories in the Fertile Crescent (the area encompassed by modern Iraq, Egypt, Jordan and Syria) and they must have been a magnificent sight, dotted as they were about the flat landscape. They rose to several hundred feet high, and were in the form of step pyramids, usually with a shrine on the top, sometimes at the side. There were usually seven steps, each one painted in the colour attributed to the planet linked to it. The most famous of these step pyramids was the Tower of Babel (Babylon): 200 tons of gold were used for decorating the shrine of the god at its summit.

Although no complete zodiac is to be found on any Babylonian sculpture, the boundary stones marking the ownership of land do show some of the zodiac constellations – notably Capricorn, a goat fish, symbolizing the rulership of the celestial god Ea (or En-ki) over the waters of the earth. Scorpio, Sagittarius and Cancer are also depicted. On Babylonian sculptures there are easily recognizable symbols of the Sun, Moon and Venus.

Astrology in Egypt

The priests of Egypt were well versed in astronomical lore from the fourth millenium BC, when the two Egyptian kingdoms were united. According to Classical writers, they were said to have been instructed in astrology by the Chaldeans (i.e. the Babylonians). They made use of their astronomical lore to arrange their all-important religious festival for New Year's Day, which was timed to coincide with the heliacal rising of Sirius, the brightest star in the heavens. The appearance of this star above the eastern horizon heralded the start of the Nile flood – as

LEFT *The sun-disc is depicted between the god and his worshippers on this Babylonian tablet commemorating the refoundation of the sun temple in Sippar (9th century BC).*

CENTRE *Symbols of the Sun, Moon, Venus and the constellation Scorpio are to be seen on this Babylonian boundary stone (c. 1120 BC).*

RIGHT *Apparently, a knowledge of the zodiac did not reach Egypt until the 3rd century BC by which time the Egyptians had assimilated Chaldean and Greek ideas and beliefs. The Zodiac is engraved on the roof of the temple of Denderah (c. 100 BC).*

important to the Egyptians as the earlier, springtime inundations of the Tigris and Euphrates were to the Babylonians.

Horoscopes have been found – but they are hieroglyphical diagrams – on cenotaphs, coffin lids, the ceilings of tombs and temples. These too are New Year's Day horoscopes. Their purpose was to serve as maps for the souls of the dead, to make it easier for them to join the Sun in his boat at the right time.

The earliest extant example of a personal horoscope is that of King Nectanebus, born in 358 BC.

The sole addition that the Egyptians made to the astronomical knowledge of the Babylonians was a solar calendar. This was a marked improvement on the Babylonian one (in fact our own calendar today is based on it). It seems too that when they regularized the twelve signs of the zodiac, apparently in the seventh century, the Babylonians gave the Egyptian name of the Ram to Aries, and the Egyptian names of the God with Streams and Two Fishes to the constellations of Aquarius and Pisces.

Astrology cannot have been applied in Egypt to the casting of individual birth horoscopes until the civilization was nearing its end – that is after the Babylonian conquest of the country in the seventh century BC.

Greek astrology

Although Thales (*c.* 639–546 BC), Pythagoras (*c.* 569–470 BC), Anaxagoras (*c.* 500–428 BC), Plato (*c.* 429–348 BC) and Eudoxus (*c.* 408–355 BC) all travelled to Egypt to discuss astronomical matters, only Thales apparently made use of his astronomical knowledge for astrological purposes, as he is said to have predicted the eclipse that determined the outcome of the struggle between the Medes and Lydians in May 585 BC.

In fact, astrology only gained popularity in Greece as a result of Alexander the Great's excursions into Asia, and the subsequent spread of the Hellenistic empire and influence. After Alexander founded Alexandria in Egypt the settling of Greeks in that country will have made them familiar with the popular astrology current in the third century BC.

However, it was an Alexandrian-born Greek who wrote the first comprehensive textbook in the second century AD. This was the famous *Tetrabiblos* of Claudius Ptolemy. He systematized astrology by dividing the constellations into groups of four elements (Fire, Earth, Air and Water) and three qualities which described their functions; the 'houses' of the horoscope (i.e. sectors relating to specific

9

ASTROLOGY

areas of activity and relationship) was another invention of Ptolemy. Yet, in spite of this, some extant horoscopes that were drawn up by Greeks in the third century AD do not attempt any detailed analysis of character, or the life prospects of the individuals concerned.

It must not be imagined that in Greece astrology was accepted uncritically. In fact, opinion among the foremost thinkers was divided. But it is clear from what he wrote in the *Timaeus* that Plato must have believed in it; and it was a Greek poet Aratus of Soli who first composed a detailed description of all the known constellations of the heaven in verse.

RIGHT A beautiful illustration of Man's relationship to the Macrocosm, taken from Les Tres Riches Heures du Duc de Berry *(15th century AD). The signs of the zodiac are shown in relationship to the parts of the body.*

The Sun in his chariot and the signs of the zodiac are shown on this Byzantine illustration (AD 820) to Ptolemy's treatise on Astrology, the Tetrabiblos.

Astrology in Rome

The Romans were quick to adopt anything that the Greeks had taken up, and astrology in Rome flourished to a greater extent than it had ever done before. From the Roman emperors downwards, anyone who could afford to was keen to have his horoscope cast. However, emperors were apt to banish astrologers from time to time when they became nervous about their own safety. Yet, the Emperor Augustus (having previously sent professional astrologers packing) made his own horoscope public, and issued a coin with his Moon sign (Capricorn) on it.

Astrology in Medieval and Renaissance times

After the fall of Rome astrology suffered its first severe testing period. For, with the growth of Christianity, astrology came under very critical examination by the Church, which was understandable, for the new religion still had to pit its strength against its pagan rivals – and in particular against the mystery cults, which mainly had their origin in Egypt.

But opinion about astrology was as divided among the Church fathers as it had been among the Greeks; it had in its favour the Biblical mention of the star of Bethlehem that heralded the Saviour's birth; and in the end the efforts of churchmen, chief among whom was St Augustine, to repress it failed.

Astrology itself became encrusted with superstitions, and too many of those who practised it dabbled also in magic, so that during the Dark Ages no scientific progress was made and it suffered from a very dubious reputation in Europe. However, in the Byzantine Empire and in the Arab countries the reverse applied; for it was to these areas that scholars went in search of learning. The Arabs in particular became skilful in mathematics, which they applied to astrology, and in the creation of scientific instruments for astronomical purposes.

An example of silver coinage issued by the Emperor Augustus depicting the sign in which the Moon was placed at the time he was born (Capricorn), though he was a Sun-Libran.

Ares. leo. sagittarius. sunt calida et sicca collerica masculina. Orientalia.

Taurus. virgo. capricornus. sunt frigida et sicca melanco lica femnina. occidentalia.

Gemini. aquarius. libra. sunt calida et humida masculina sanguinea. occidentalia.

Cancer. scor pius. pisces. sunt frigida et humi da flemmatica femni na. Septentrionalia.

11

Halley's comet (which flashed across the heavens in 1066 AD) shown on the Bayeux tapestry.

Many famous astrologers practised their art during medieval and Renaissance times. Reproductions of the books they wrote on the subject are still available to this day in shops specializing in occult literature. Among these astrologers was John of Holywood, a professor of mathematics who in the thirteenth century wrote the first astrological textbook available in western Europe. At the same time the chaplain and physician to Pope Urban IV – who was also a mathematician – devised a new system for dividing the 'houses' (or sections of the horoscope). Another system was put forward in the fifteenth century by a professor of astronomy, Johann Müller, known as Regiomontanus.

Most famous of all, however, was Michael Nostradamus, born in 1503 in Saint Rémy, Provence. He was a doctor who also practised astrology. But his famous predictions would seem to have been the result of second sight as much as astrological prediction, for he gives no clue as to what astrological data might have prompted them.

With the coming of the Renaissance, learning once again flourished in Europe, and this worked to the benefit of astronomy more than astrology; for this was the time of the great scientific revolution, when Copernicus proved that the earth moved round the sun, not vice versa; and the Aristotelian dictum to the reverse was revealed as a complete error of deduction. It was assumed that this would destroy any belief in astrology; for astrologers had, of course, accepted the Aristotelian theory. In actual fact, it is immaterial which body revolves around which – this makes absolutely no difference to the accuracy of astrological analysis and prediction; but the scientists would not be convinced of this.

However, though many astrologers made names for themselves during and after the Renaissance period, no further advance was made in astrological technique from the sixteenth to the nineteenth century, and once again astrology gradually sank into decline.

Instead, it was the turn of the astronomers to make further headway, benefitting as they did from much more sophisticated equipment. The telescope had been invented by Galileo in the seventeenth century, so that closer observation could be made of the constellations and planets and new facts were discovered about them.

After the Renaissance

Bigger and better telescopes were made from the seventeenth century onwards; more detailed celestial atlases could now be drawn up. More and more, scientific knowledge increased the scope of astronomy, and popular opinion became more and more averse to its twin sister, astrology.

The astrologer, once a revered and very powerful figure from Antiquity to the time of the Renaissance, suffered an increasing loss of prestige. That is, in the West.

Astrology in the East and in the New World

In Antiquity, astrology had spread eastwards as well as westwards. In India and China it achieved great importance, though the names of the signs of the zodiac and the techniques of practice differed from those of the West. But in the Middle East and the Far East astrology still maintains its popularity (even though it was recently banned for a time in India). But this could be because of a fundamental difference in outlook on life of the peoples of the East and West. We in the West have become, if anything, too scientifically minded – with the result that religion is very much on the decline. In the East, however, the attitude is much more spiritual; and it is doubtful whether the advance of science would ever alter this situation. For the people of the East it is possible to accept both scientific truth and still hold fast to beliefs that cannot be verified by scientific tests.

Astrology not only spread to the Far East, but developed in the Americas. The Mayans of Mexico created a huge stone calendar, still to be seen, which is replete with astrological symbols. From it they were able to predict eclipses and other astronomical phenomena with a very high degree of accuracy. In Mexico, too, are to be found astronomical observatories that bear some resemblance to the step pyramids of Mesopotamia.

Astrology today

Once again, astrology seems to be going through a resurgent phase, and for the first time in several centuries it is attracting the interest of scientists. This is because the scientists themselves are being forced to re-examine many of their ideas. New facts about the universe have been discovered; theories about the moon were disproved once the astronauts stepped on it and brought back moon samples. In 1980 much excitement was produced by the photographs sent back by the NASA probe directed to pass within close range of Saturn.

There is not space available in this brief summary of the history of astrology to enlarge upon recent developments in science as they affect astronomy; but what is of special interest to astrologers is the scientific discovery of biological rhythms that can be electrically recorded, as these appear to have some connection with solar, lunar and planetary rhythms. It is known that the incidence of sun-spot cycles has an effect (or shall we say a correlationship) on economic fluctuations.

BELOW *The mathematician and astrologer Nicholas Kratzer to whom Henry VIII turned for advice (portrait by Hans Holbein).*

RIGHT *An instrument for calculating horoscopes. Each arm represents a planet that can be adjusted to its position in the zodiac at the time for which the horoscope is drawn up.*

Radiations emanating from space are now known to have differing intensity according to the positions of various stars. When the sun is below the horizon no solar X-rays or ultra-violet rays can reach that area of the earth where the sun no longer shines. Certain planets seem to be transmitters of specific radiations from space to the earth's surface.

The spirit of exploration is very much alive in today's serious astrologers; and they have been busy applying the results of their careful study of empirical data to test their theories. Evidence that militates in favour of astrological theories and beliefs is today much more liable to receive serious attention – even to the extent that radio and television programmes are slanted differently from what they were as recently as ten years ago.

Having been a practising astrologer for over forty years, it is particularly heartening to me to see the active and intelligent interest displayed by the college and university students, and other young adults of today because, having the benefit of a more advanced scientific education than people of my own generation, they have all the more chance of solving the astrological problems that have so far defeated our efforts.

To end this very brief history of astrology, it might interest readers who have no knowledge of the subject to have a brief outline of the technical details and the significance of an individual birth chart.

THE INDIVIDUAL HOROSCOPE

This should be calculated for the date, month, year, and also the time of day or night, of the person's birth. With the use of 'ephemerides', books of astronomical tables of the motions of the sun, moon and planets year by year, and also a 'Table of houses', which enables the astrologer to place the planets in their right signs and in the right positions in the divisions ('houses') of the horoscope, an analysis and synthesis of the chart can then be made.

Signs, planets and houses all have symbolical meanings, as follows:

Signs

ARIES 'The Ram': a symbol of unrestrained energy, indicative of a love of action for its own sake; predisposed towards impulsiveness, courage, and an urge for leadership and conquest; linked with the principle of dynamic energy

TAURUS 'The Bull': symbolic of steadfastness, reliability, practicality, patience and perseverance; but inclines to limitations of mental outlook, interests and aptitudes; connected with the principle of conservation

GEMINI 'The Twins': symbolic of agility, versatility, adaptability; it is connected with the principle of communication and, is especially associated with mental ingenuity

CANCER 'The Crab': indicative of sensitivity, caution, retentiveness, and also with the principle of protection and nourishment; the sign associated with the maternal and domestic qualities

LEO 'The Lion': symbolic of controlled energy, used methodically; organizing ability; instinctively wields authority

VIRGO 'The Virgin': symbolic of perfectionism attained through meticulous attention to detail; so connected with the principle of discrimination

LIBRA 'The Balance': as the symbol suggests, it is linked with equilibrium; has a well-balanced outlook on life, and an instinct for identifying with one's environment

SCORPIO 'The Scorpion': intensely emotional people, hypersensitive in their reactions to everyone and everything, but also very analytical

SAGITTARIUS 'The Archer': symbolic of expansiveness, a desire to explore, expressed in generosity, love of adventure, willingness to take chances

CAPRICORN 'The Goat': symbolic of inflexibility, perpetuity; excessively ambitious

AQUARIUS 'The Water-Bearer': symbolic of humanitarianism; also of non-attachment expressed through impartiality; also connected with the principle of progress through experimentation

PISCES 'The Fishes': symbolic of change. They are also very dependent on help from others to bring out the best in themselves

The Planets

SUN: associated with the principle of integration
MOON: symbolic of responsiveness, reflection
MERCURY: associated with the principle of communication
VENUS: associated with the principle of beauty, harmony, unity
MARS: associated with the principle of aggression, combativeness expressed in physical action
JUPITER: symbolic of faith, optimism, expansion
SATURN: symbolic of restraint, rigidity
URANUS: symbolic of nonconformity, individuality
NEPTUNE: symbolic of illusion, delusion, dissolution
PLUTO: symbol of elimination

Houses

1 The personality
2 Acquisitions gained by own effort – earnings
3 Mental outlook; relationships with members of family other than parents or grandparents; short-distance travel
4 Symbolic of domestic background; mother
5 Creative potential; romantic relationship; offspring
6 Personal health; working surroundings, conditions, nature of work
7 Partnership in particular; relationships with people in general
8 Shared interests; commitments
9 Long-distance travel; spirituality
10 Status, more especially career status
11 Friendships; cherished aims
12 Seclusion; retreat; that which is most private to the person concerned.

The analysis and synthesis of a horoscope are made by relating the solar, lunar and planetary positions to each other, to the houses they occupy, and the signs they are in. The meanings of signs, planets and houses listed above have to be aligned with the matters under consideration; thus, to judge what the individual's career aptitudes and prospects might be, it would be necessary to take into consideration the individual's character, which can only be assessed by an interpretation of the *whole* pattern of the chart; the personality; the first house and any planet in or 'ruling' that house; the second house (financial prospects); and lastly, both sixth and tenth houses, as both will give some clues as to the preferable type of occupation, or the role most suitable for the person.

Rulerships

As there are twelve houses of the horoscope and, including Sun and Moon, only ten stellar bodies, it is obvious that not all houses can be occupied by a planet; several may be in one house. In which case, those that happen to be empty can also be 'interpreted' in terms of the planet ruling the sign that has been lined up with the house.

Flowers associated with the following signs:

ARIES – Wild Cherry	LEO – Sorrel	SAGITTARIUS – Chicory
TAURUS – Common Burdock	VIRGO – Valerian	CAPRICORN – Knapweed
GEMINI – Marsh Marigold	LIBRA – Dandelion	AQUARIUS – Lady's Slipper
CANCER – Honeysuckle	SCORPIO – Wormwood	PISCES – Saxifrage

ARIES 'THE RAM'

Birth period 21 March–20 April

Robust is the operative word to describe the Aries personality. People born under this sign exude tremendous vitality. Life is a glorious adventure for Arians: they crave excitement and they make sure that they get plenty of it. Always eager for new experiences, and ready to face up to any challenge, Arians lead very full lives. Other types may be content to wait for opportunities to get ahead, but Aries believes it is up to him or her to create those opportunities, and initiative and enterprise are two of the most prominent characteristics in the Arian's make up.

The principle characteristic of Aries is that of spontaneous combustion, so it is no wonder that the true Arian is so impetuous and so unrestrained in behaviour. Action is the breath of life to Aries; and, when in action, Aries is jet-propelled. Wildly enthusiastic about whoever or whatever is the current focus of attention, Aries seems to become oblivious of everything else: singlemindedness is yet another trait in the Aries nature.

Driving force, self-assurance and ambition are the strongest traits of Aries and keep Arians well out in front in the 'rat race'.

Courageous to the point of being foolhardy, Aries is always ready to take risks to attain an objective; and in times of war it is Aries who will be prominent among those awarded medals for valour. A trail-blazer, too, Aries will be the first to go where no one had dared to go before: it is a pity that today there are so few areas of the globe that provide an outlet for Aries to brave the perils of the unknown, for Arians are the pioneers of the zodiac.

Mentally, Arians are imaginative and at times brilliantly creative, but not deeply reflective. They are too impatient to spend much time pondering over anything. Once they make up their minds about a subject, they are very firm in their convictions and will argue fiercely to defend them; but they are no match for people skilled in the art of debate. Apt to jump to conclusions far too quickly, Arians often lack sound judgment and do not take kindly at all to people who point this out. The fact is that Arians see things only from their own point of view, for they can be so wrapped up in their own affairs that they take little interest in those of other people.

There is no guile in Arians and they speak their minds frankly and make their motives very clear to others. They would consider it beneath their dignity to employ underhand methods to gain their ends. But tact is not one of the Aries attributes; in fact, they are apt to be forthright to the point of being much too outspoken. Very quick-tempered, in the heat of the moment Arians will say more than they mean – and find it difficult to apologize for this. On the other hand, Aries is never one to bear a grudge or be vindictive.

Emotionally, this type is very ardent, passionate in love, extremely loyal to the people for whom they have respect and affection. But tolerance is not one of the Aries qualities – Arians are very critical of other people's failings. Most of all, they despise weakness: it seems to bring out the worst in their nature. They respect those who stand up against them, and have little time for those who can be easily intimidated.

There is a very romantic streak in the Arian, who falls in love on sight, and idealizes the object of his affections. This is the type who rushes into marriage. But, in view of what has already been said of the Aries character, it is not surprising that partnerships are apt to follow a troubled course; for Arians can be much too domineering, much too possessive towards the people with whom they become closely involved.

Aries is usually somewhat more accident-prone than the rest of the zodiac. But accidents are more usually the result of carelessness, haste, and wilful disregard of safety precautions than other causes. Aries likes to use tools, but though skilful with them, still manages to suffer mishaps. Aries also loves weapons – he will take great pride in his skill as a marksman. Most of all, the true Arian loves sport, especially the more dangerous kinds. You will find the Arian on the race track, the speed track and everywhere else where energetic sport is in progress, and at some time or other in life the Aries-born are likely to acquire a scar on head or face. But when Arians take to the dance floor, watch out: here they are seldom in their element, and the poor partner suffers from having toes crushed by those clumsy Aries feet.

Travel has a tremendous appeal for Arians: they prefer the more out-of-the-way places. The outdoors has a great attraction for them, and when indoors they will keep the windows open even in the coldest weather. However, there will be plenty of heating to counteract the cold blasts – for Aries craves warmth as well as fresh air. This is the type that loves to sit before an open fire rather than to heat the home with gas or electrical heating appliances. And why not? After all, Aries is a 'Fire' sign and the Arian feels an affinity with the leaping flames of a brightly burning fire.

The Aries Man

Aries is a go-getter who will let nothing stand in his way. When faced with obstructions, he tackles them head-on: rather like his namesake, the ram. Even when walking, this resemblance to the ram can be seen in the way he seems to project himself forward head first. And, like the ram, the Aries man often has locks of hair curling crisply over his temples like horns. Other physical resemblances to the ram are to be traced in the facial structure of the Arian man such as the shape of the nose and positioning of the eyes.

He is a 'man's man', and if you are his girlfriend or wife you must accept the fact that he will probably spend as much, if not more, of his spare time with his male cronies than with you. He is at his best in male company, and very popular with his own sex, despite

17

the fact that he can be quarrelsome, overbearing, and very self-centred.

A careerist by temperament, Aries is especially suited for hazardous or physically exacting occupations. Professionally, he will do particularly well in the defence services (especially the Army) or the police force; makes a good politician but a poor diplomat; is quite happy in the higher branches of the Civil Service, despite the fact that this involves adhering to routine; often finds his niche in the Foreign Office, which provides scope for work abroad. Engineering is something in which he excels, too. Pyrotechnics, surgery, and ophthalmics are other occupations that seem to have an especial appeal for him. And he is completely happy if he takes up farming, or breeding or training horses. In the world of commerce and industry, Aries is to be found at the head of companies; and this type often becomes a business promoter. The constructional trades and industries are especially suitable for Aries. But no true Arian will make a successful banker, for he is not sufficiently interested in money to make the manipulation of it his career. Generous to the point of being extravagant, Aries believes that money should circulate freely.

ties but should moderate this, as when under the influence of alcohol he can become aggressive.

He is the sort of man who smokes a pipe in preference to cigarettes or a cigar; usually has a dog at his heels and, if a country dweller, a rifle under his arm; he looks his best in tweeds – and uniforms (the only time he wears a hat is usually when it is part of a uniform).

The Aries Woman

The Aries woman probably upholds the female liberation movement, but has no need to, as she can always make her way ahead in a man's world. Men like her because there is a masculine streak in her personality, even though she has all the feminine characteristics as well. She can think like a man, though her feelings are those of a woman – and a very romantic, ardent one. When in love, she will sacrifice all for romance; but she, like her male counterpart, is also a careerist by temperament, and this can lead to problems if she marries the type of partner who expects her to remain at home. Truth to tell, the Aries woman is not very interested in domesticity; she prefers to engage someone else to run her home efficiently while she employs her talents elsewhere.

Aries man often has locks of hair curling crisply over his temples . . . is a go-getter who will let nothing stand in his way.

Happiest when self-employed, Aries does not always make a success of working partnerships – unless the other party is content to remain a sleeping partner. As boss, Aries will be tough, but fair, with his labour force; he drives himself hard, and expects those who work for him to do likewise.

When Aries turns to reading, his preferences are for biographies, adventure stories, travel books and sporting literature. Pop music may appeal to him, and so may classical music of the Wagnerian type. His taste in food veers towards the exotic and he prefers savouries to sweet dishes; he enjoys drinking alcohol in large quanti-

She can be very jealous in her attitude to her male partner – woe betide him if he casts an eye in other directions, but she is very loyal and even if marriage turns out badly, will not engage in any liaisons to compensate for this. Her attitude is that if the partnership is not working out well, then let us make a clean break.

She can be a good friend to others of her own sex, but is apt to be a bit too 'bossy' and rather too keen to tell them how to run their lives. As a parent, she maintains strict discipline over her children, but gives them plenty of encouragement to become self-reliant. She is especially proud of her sons, but may find it difficult to get on so

Aries woman can always make her way ahead in a man's world and is not very interested in domesticity and prefers to engage someone else to run her home efficiently. She is very romantic.

well with her daughters when they pass beyond childhood. Conversely, it is the Aries man who spoils his daughters and is tough on his sons, however proud he is of them.

The Aries woman likes to keep well up with fashion, and looks her best in simple, well-cut clothes. She is the type who can wear slacks to perfection, for – if typical of her sign – she is slim. Joan Crawford was very typical in appearance, manner and character of her Aries Sun sign. Bette Davies, though physically less typical, strongly demonstrates the Aries psychological characteristics: the way in which she fought the film bosses in order to maintain her independence is typically Arian.

The Aries Child

The Aries child has a simple, uncomplicated nature; he or she will be something of a handful for parents and teachers, for right from infancy Aries children make it very clear that they have a will of their own and that they are determined to gain plenty of attention from everyone around them. Boisterous in play, and given to tantrums, these children need firm handling – but also should be given a fair measure of liberty to think and act for themselves. You can send Aries children to boarding school without any fear that they will pine for home as they are not the clinging type.

Very competitive in spirit, Aries children are keen to do well in examinations, and very keen to take the lead in all the social and sporting activities that are part of school life. But they should be taught to take more care of their possessions, to cultivate tidy habits, and to curb their destructive impulses. When angry, the Aries child becomes violent: mothers of Aries boys are wise to keep a first-aid kit handy to bandage cuts and to deal with bruises incurred by small sons who will not learn that they should not take on boys bigger than themselves.

The Aries girl is something of a tomboy who prefers the company of boys to that of other girls; she is very keen to show that anything they can do she can do better. Her tastes in toys does not include dolls but rather the kind of toys her brother chooses. She does well at sports, but such things as needlework will not appeal to her.

Both boys and girls have a strong sex drive, and never lack for friends of the opposite sex. But, in youth (and indeed throughout life) Arians fall out of love as rapidly as they fall into it, so be prepared for a rapid succession of boyfriends if you have Aries daughters.

Aries children are seldom ill, but when ailing run very high temperatures: this is nature's way of helping them to 'burn out' any maladies. The parts of the body connected with this sign of the zodiac are the head, the nerves of the face, the kidneys and bladder. Nervous or emotional stress will bring on minor kidney or bladder complaints; and also very acute headaches which can become migraines. At some time or other in life the Aries-born are likely to acquire a scar on head or face.

19

The Aries child is boisterous in play and given to tantrums.

Affinities of Aries

The people with whom Arians seem most in tune are those born at these times of the year:

LEO (23 July–22 August)

SAGITTARIUS (23 November–22 December)

LIBRA (23 September–22 October) is the sign opposite to Aries, and very often marriages occur between the two; this is a particularly good combination for various reasons. Librans can bring influence to bear on Aries, in their own tactful way, to modify some of the too-extremist qualities of the Aries nature. With the help of Libra, Aries can learn to become more patient, more tolerant, more able to see other people's points of view. However, it will be a miracle if Libra ever manages to persuade Aries to accept compromises, for they are anathema to them. Arians can instil more self-confidence into Librans, and encourage them to take a firm stand at times when it is vital to do so.

GEMINI (21 May–20 June). The Geminian's lively ways, bright ideas, adaptability and sense of humour appeal to Aries. Both Aries and Gemini have something child-like in their attitude to life, and both retain the spirit of youth throughout life.

People with whom Aries may find it especially difficult to keep on good terms are those born at these times of the year:

CANCER (21 June–22 July). Aries becomes intensely irritated with the cautious attitude of Cancer, and the moody ways of these subjects and their tendency to be secretive at times.

CAPRICORN (23 December–20 January). Much too conservative and phlegmatic for Arian taste. Capricorn throws cold water on the enthusiasm and vitality of Aries.

AQUARIUS (21 January–19 February). Aries is fascinated by Aquarians, but infuriated, so detached.

TAURUS 'THE BULL'

Birth period 21 April–20 May

'Beware of the Bull' reads the sign nailed to the gate of the field in which a magnificent specimen has raised his head from grazing to return your gaze. Yet, unless you are foolish enough to provoke his wrath, you stand in no peril from him. For the bull, like the cow, is a placid creature. If you doubt this, witness the way he will allow himself to be led around the ring at a cattle show for the benefit of the spectators. There is no trace of nervousness; in fact, he appears very docile – but that is because the man in charge of him allows him to move at his own pace and handles him gently.

It is the same with people born under this sign of the zodiac. Taureans are by nature peace-loving, very amiable people who desire to live in harmony with their associates. You will not find Taureans stirring up trouble; in fact, they will do all in their power to avoid it. However, if you try their patience too much you could regret it. For, once aroused to anger, this type is formidable. Once you have deeply angered or deeply hurt the Taurean, he or she will be slow to forgive and slower still to forget what has happened. The danger signals to look out for are unmistakable. A Taurus man begins to move his head slowly from side to side, and drums a tattoo on the floor with his foot; a Taurus woman also starts to tap the floor with her foot (and a very dainty foot it is too, for both men and women have very small feet in proportion to their bodies).

Taurus is a 'fixed' and 'earthy' sign. Taureans are very consistent in outlook, habits, behaviour – never inclined to do anything on the spur of the moment, very averse to change so long as their circumstances suit them; very firm in their opinions and convictions, and very practical in their attitude to life. The Taurean is not one to 'dream the impossible dream' or to yearn for the unattainable: any fantasizing will be along lines well within the bounds of possibility, for Taurus is a realist; that is, so far as the material side of life is concerned. In this respect, people born under the sign of the Bull have a very keen sense of relative values.

However, Venus is the planetary ruler of Taurus, and Venus is the planet of love. Where affairs of the heart are concerned, there is a very romantic side to the Taurean nature. Fortunately it is kept within bounds, so that although Taurus may fall in love with someone who would be a most undesirable marriage partner, he or she will have the good sense to look elsewhere when it is time to settle down. That is not to say that Taureans are cold-blooded types who will reject love for money or social position; rather it is that they are usually fortunate enough to meet someone with whom they are in affinity and who is also of the same practical turn of mind. That is why divorce is less common among Taureans than many of the other zodiac types; they do not marry in haste, so they seldom have reason to repent at leisure. Though Taureans demand absolute fidelity from their partners, they cannot resist the occasional opportunity to indulge in a mild flirtation elsewhere. It is, however,

a very harmless one: Taurus is very loyal.

Taureans are not particularly enterprising, for they are too cautious to take chances; this can be a handicap, for it means that they do not always exploit their capabilities to the full, or give themselves the chance of finding out whether they have more talents than they realize. Taurus has a flair for astute bargaining – and the infinite patience necessary for it. When Taureans take on the role of agent, they will get the best price for the people they are acting for.On the other hand, if Taurus is not the type to launch out on experiments, it is the people born under this sign who will put what others initiate on a very firm basis, and keep it that way. Taurus has excellent administrative ability. Moreover, this type is well fitted to hold superior positions: Taureans are able to keep on very good terms with their subordinates because, though firm in exercising authority, they are not domineering.

Taureans prefer the types of occupation that offer steady advancement and long-range security. This is the sign that has to do with money, and Taureans are excellent at handling finance; which is why so many become bankers or financiers. Taurus believes in making money work for itself, and invests wisely. One of the first things the average Taurean will invest in is a home of his own, preferably with some land attached to it, sufficient to build on as well as provide a garden. Many Taureans make a business career in this area, either going into the building trade, becoming an estate agent or training to become an architect or interior decorator.

The broad range of occupations that are most likely to attract the Taureans includes the fashion and beauty industries as well as the arts (many have considerable musical talent, and it is very rare to find a Taurean who lacks an appreciation for music; the Taurean will never begrudge money spent on concerts or the opera).

As Taurus is an earthy and 'fruitful' sign, agriculture and floriculture appeal to people born under it. They have the gardener's traditional 'green fingers'. They are country-lovers who revel in the beauties of nature; as landscape gardeners no other zodiac type can excel them.

Family life means a great deal to the Taurus-born, and as our roots lie deep in our family backgrounds, for a Taurean to have to pull up those roots would be a particularly traumatic experience. That is not to say they always get on well with relatives – but they will always stand by them in times of trouble. However, if you have a Taurean relative do not expect him or her to be a soft touch. If they advance you money it will be on the same business basis as for people outside the family. Taurus is perfectly prepared to mix sentiment with business, so long as the two can be kept in balance.

Taureans are good at creating a really comfortable as well as attractive domestic background for themselves and their families. Ultra-modern, austere, perfectly functional (and possibly hideous) modern furniture will

not be tolerated in the Taurean home. If it is up-to-date, it must also be very pleasing to the eye. Taureans prefer solid furniture – just as well as most of them are sturdily built, and their chairs and beds should be constructed accordingly. However, the real reason for their preference for the heavier type of furniture is that it adds to their feeling of security.

There are always plenty of plants (especially flower-bearing varieties) in the Taurean home. Even if Taureans reside in the heart of a city the chances are that they will choose to live where they can be reminded of the country, if only because a square or a park, or at least some grass verges and trees, are close to the house or block of flats. Even if forced to dwell in those high-rise monstrosities erected over the past twenty years or so, the window boxes adorning the ledges, and the tubs and shrubs on the balconies, will be a sign that Taureans are determined to keep in touch with nature.

Throat, neck-glands are the vulnerable bodily parts of the Taurean. This is a very fertile sign, so women born under it are probably particularly grateful for modern contraceptive methods.

Physically, people born under this sign bear the hallmark of Venus: the large, soft, velvet eyes of Venus, and the full, rounded neck.

whom he does not come in daily contact through his work. Persuade him to join local clubs; share his enthusiasm for good music; but let him off the leash to spend at least one evening a week in the sole company of his male pals – for he is as much a man's man as attracted to the opposite sex, and he is too well-mannered to indulge in racy conversation with men while in the company of women. Bear in mind that he is very particular about the behaviour of the woman he has chosen to be his mate, and act out the feminine role to the full when it comes to turning on the charm, plying him with flattery. Be wary of showing too much liking for his male friends, though: he has a very jealous nature, and is apt to misconstrue the most harmless flirtatious gambits on your part.

He will not be mean with the housekeeping allowance, but he will want to be assured that you get good value for it, and keep strict account of how you spend it. You can always count on him to fork out willingly for additions to your wardrobe, for he likes to see you stylishly dressed, and approves of your efforts to be well groomed in other respects. He too takes pride in his appearance. But if a typical Taurean he is apt to develop a weight problem, partly because he is lazy about taking exercise. You will have to encourage him to correct this fault: references to other overweight males, rather than to his own bulk, will spur him into keeping fit.

The Taurean man loves his comfort, food, and music but must be encouraged to avoid weight problems.

The Taurus Man

Manliness is the chief characteristic of the Taurean male: he is the kind of man who makes a wonderful husband, providing his wife makes a fuss of him and remembers that he loves his comfort and takes a very keen interest in food; the kind of man who becomes a connoisseur of wine; but who does not become a boor or a bully when under the influence of alcohol; slow to anger, in any case, but when aroused his fury will make you tremble – so do not provoke your placid Taurean mate to the point where his patience and good humour are exhausted.

He likes his home run on methodical lines, as he does everything else; and you can count on him to stick to regular habits. For his own good, though, encourage him to make new acquaintances among people with

The Taurus Woman

Very curvaceous physically but even if she is very slim in youth, the Taurean woman is likely to grow plumper as the years pass. This being a sign ruled by Venus, she is certainly a 'good looker' – and very attractive to the opposite sex. The Taurus woman is a sensual creature who really enjoys lovemaking and needs physical fulfilment if she is to be happy in marriage. For one thing, lack of attention on her husband's part is very demoralizing to the Taurean woman; and he will only have himself to blame if she turns elsewhere for consolation. She is, by temperament, very faithful but at the same time has

The Taurean woman is very curvaceous physically, likes an aperitif before dinner, but give her plenty of time to get ready if you intend to take her out for the evening.

no intention of allowing her partner to take her physical charms for granted – so she will make him aware that other men find her attractive.

The Taurean wife is a lazy housewife at times; she is inclined to put off as long as possible the more tedious, unappealing household chores. But she is a wonderful hostess when entertaining and very generous in providing hospitality for guests.

If and when she is feeling at odds with the world around her, music will do wonders to restore her to her usual amiable mood; so will a little tipple from the right bottle. Taurean women look forward to what, a few decades ago, used to be called the cocktail hour; and she still likes an aperitif before dining. So if you are married to a Taurean spouse, make a pleasant little ritual of exchanging the day's gossip with her over a drink when you return home every evening. But do give her plenty of time to get ready if you intend to take her out for the evening: she just cannot hurry over her *toilette*, but the result will more than compensate you for waiting patiently for her to complete it.

The Taurus Child

It should be a fairly painless business rearing your young Taurean; for right from infancy you will discover that, providing your child is subjected to a regular routine, he or she will be good-tempered, and very responsive to affectionate attention. But any disturbance of routine badly upsets this type of child.

Once at the crawling and toddling stages, there is no reason for you to feel (as so many hard-pressed mothers feel) that you need eyes in the back of your head to keep track of what the Taurean infant is up to. So long as you

give this child some bricks to play with he or she will remain contentedly occupied with them; this is the constructive instinct showing itself at a very early stage. And, you will notice that the little Taurean, even while a very young baby, seems to appreciate the sound of music, especially the more soothing kind. Once he or she has learned to speak, it will not be long before you find this child crooning away and soon the name of every tune heard on the radio will be stored up in the Taurean memory.

On the other hand, do not be surprised if your little Taurean seems to be a slow developer in other respects. It takes Taureans that much longer to get a firm grasp of anything they try to learn. Similarly, though you will go through the teething period with this child without being subjected to pandemonium in the household, with everyone else's nerves frayed by excessive childish wails of distress, you may become rather anxious because your Taurus baby shows no inclination to stand upright at the usual age for this to happen. Taureans like to feel very sure of their footing, which is why they feel nervous when walking on soft surfaces. And just try getting them into a boat! They will choose any other form of transport (even air travel, to which they are certainly not addicted) rather than trust themselves to be carried anywhere by water. In fact, they will not venture onto a pier if they can avoid doing so!

Taureans can be led, but never driven, so it is no use trying to force a Taurus child to do what goes against the grain; but with a little guile you can always overcome Taurean obstinacy. The trick is to appeal to the child's good nature and good sense. If you adopt a sympathetic attitude to his objections, a little flattery, blended with a request rather than a command, the Taurean child can be persuaded to change his mind.

This type of child is inclined to become too possessive – of his or her toys, of your affection, and of the attention of playmates. Jealousy as well as acquisitiveness are basic traits in the Taurean personality, and the child needs to be helped to bring both under control. So encourage him or her to share with others what they most value.

Once at school, your Taurean child will make steady if not spectacular headway after settling into the routine and discipline there. Out of school, see to it that Taureans cultivate hobbies as they tend to lapse into idleness when at a loose end.

One last point regarding education. It will probably be wiser to send your Taurean son or daughter to a one-sex school rather than a co-educational one. Why? Well, even while still at nursery school age, you will observe that your little Taurean is very strongly attracted to playmates of the opposite sex (and very attractive to them, too). This could become a source of problems when Taureans reach teenage years – for one thing it will take their mind off their studies if they become too friendly with the members of the opposite sex they mingle with during school hours.

The Taurean child appreciates the sound of music and given some bricks to play with will remain happy.

Affinities of Taurus

People with whom Taureans are particularly in affinity seem to be those born at these times of the year:

CANCER (21 June–22 July). Another home-loving type with whom Taurus shares an interest in cooking: both types make an art of it.

VIRGO (23 August–22 September). The rational outlook on life of this type is much in keeping with the Taurean.

CAPRICORN (23 December–20 January). Taurus admires Capricornians for their ambition and stamina, which is akin to that of Taurus.

PISCES (20 February–20 March). Despite the weaknesses of the Piscean, Taurus has a very tender spot for the children of the Fishes. This is because Pisces is so sympathetic, so affectionate. And the Pisceans boost the Taurean's ego with their admiration for the sons and daughters of the Bull. Besides, Pisces is very romantic, and this is another bond between the two.

Taureans tend to get on less well with the following:

SCORPIO (23 October–22 November) is the opposite sign to Taurus; and both Taurus and Scorpio have a strong sex drive. As marriage partners, they are ideally suited from the physical point of view; but sometimes Taurus feels that the Scorpio is being a bit too possessive, even though this is very flattering. 'And what about you?' the Scorpio may well retort. There is, however, a great difference between the grades of jealousy of the Taurean and the Scorpio person: in the latter it can become an obsession, and a very dangerous one. Not so with the Taurean.

Taureans find it difficult to get on with the following:

AQUARIUS (21 January–19 February). Taurus may not feel at ease with Aquarians; for one thing, they are too detached, unpredictable and poor Taurus cannot make head or tail of their erratic behaviour.

LEO (23 July–22 August). Leos make the Taurean see red at times for they want to dominate the scene – and Taurus has no intention of being overshadowed by their exhibitionism.

LIBRA (23 September–22 October). It is an odd thing, but though both Libra and Taurus are ruled by Venus, Taurus feels a little uneasy in the company of Libra. Why? Librans are such strategists, and Taureans sense that they are being skilfully manipulated by these charming people. Also, Librans can be a bit unreliable when the going is tough – they disappear until friends or associates are out of trouble – and this is something that Taurus would never do.

ARIES (21 March–20 April) and GEMINI (21 May–20 June). As for these, the former is too provocative, too quick to argue or quarrel, too jet-propelled; the latter is too restless, too inconsistent, too much of a light-weight, for the liking of Taurus.

SAGITTARIUS (23 November–22 December). Last, but not least, the Sagittarian should also be mentioned. The grand scale on which Sagittarians do everything, their happy-go-lucky ways and their temperamental moods, are frowned upon by Taurus. Sagittarians none-theless fascinate Taurus because they add great zest to any surroundings in which they are to be found; and Taurus, being very sociable and fond of merry company, appreciates this.

GEMINI "THE TWINS"

Birth period 21 May–20 June

Mercury, which orbits the sun more rapidly than any other of the planets, is ruler of Gemini, the sign of the zodiac that has to do with communication. The dictionary definition of the term mercurial is that of a person who is volatile, sprightly, ready-witted. And that is certainly true of the typical Geminian. Geminians have a strong compulsion to keep on the move as much as possible, and when in motion they certainly cover the ground at a very fast pace. Their favourite form of transport is, as might be expected, the aeroplane – for was not Mercury the winged messenger of the gods? (Their Sun sign is an 'Air' element sign.) Insatiably curious, they endeavour to keep tabs on all that is going on around them, and are always ready to take a hand in other people's affairs. It irks Gemini to feel excluded, just as it is galling for the person born under this sign to find that other people around them are more up-to-date on news and events than they are. Very quick on the uptake, equally quick to seize opportunities to try their hand at anything new, Geminians are noted for their adaptability and versatility: but not for their singleness of purpose or powers of concentration. Both need to be deliberately cultivated, otherwise, even though they are very intelligent and have more creative potential than many of the other zodiac types, they will be unable to make the most of their talents because they spread themselves in too many different directions, fail to follow through what they take up. Another handicap is a tendency to become too bogged down with the petty details of what they are dealing with at the moment and to be sidetracked by them.

Love of communication breeds a love of language, and Geminians, who are voracious readers, acquire an ability to express themselves both vividly and wittily: they have a wonderful sense of humour. You will find yourself enraptured by this and by their eloquence – for a while, anyway; but inevitably there comes the time when you want to put cotton wool in your ears to gain a respite from the voice that goes on and on – and on. Be a bit sceptical when they assume an air of profound wisdom about the subject you are discussing with them, as the chances are that they have only a superficial acquaintance with what they talk about so authoritatively. Gemini is always out to impress, and hates to admit ignorance when appealed to for superior knowledge. This could account also for the Geminian tendency to embroider the truth even when it serves no useful purpose to do so. Certainly your Geminian is not above telling lies in order to extricate him or herself from trouble. But when they use their lively imagination to good purpose, Geminians can be very creative, whether in a literary sense or in other ways. Innovation comes naturally to this type.

Do not try arguing with a Geminian – it will get you nowhere but into a state of mental confusion, for Gemini will skilfully sidetrack you just when you think you have proved your point.

Geminians have lots of charm when they care to turn it on, though they are apt to be a bit too gushing when it comes to paying compliments and enthusing over anything. But they can also be very sarcastic: it is their weapon when anyone irritates them. As a rule, though so physically energetic, Geminians are not given to wreaking physical violence on people who arouse them to anger. They will not start a punch-up, or even kick the dog or hurl plates or other objects to relieve their feelings; but they will find a noisy way of doing so by engaging in some form of manual labour which they will perform with the maximum amount of din. It is just another way of telling you what they think of you.

Geminians are not to be relied on in times of emergency, for they have a highly sensitive nervous system that collapses under strain. At such times they are apt to go to pieces, showing signs of hysteria. On the other hand, they are quite clever at doing several things at once – for theirs is a dual sign. The duality shows up in other, paradoxical, ways: in their inconsistency – they change their minds, their points of view, their aims and intentions, with lightning rapidity. Gemini is the sign of the twins: however, these are not identical twins, but twins of opposite sexes. This is a graphic way of symbolizing the interplay of mind and feelings of Geminians. When giving way to their feelings, they act on instinct; at other times they will be cool, calculating, completely rational and objective in attitude. Because they are mercurial by nature, they are not given to moods of deep reflection or long-sustained intense feelings about anyone or anything.

This lack of emotional depth makes it easier for them to handle personal relationships. Friendly in spirit, very gregarious by nature, the type is quick to make acquaintances who become friends; but Gemini does not become passionately attached to friends, because he or she lacks the need to feel emotionally secure. In fact, if relationships show signs of becoming too binding, the Geminian will seek to escape from them. Geminians take romance lightly, enjoy the art of flirtation, tend to have several strings to their bow. Actually, the people for whom they most care are probably their relatives, but Gemini will not allow family ties to restrict his or her personal freedom. So far as friendships are concerned, out of sight is out of mind with Geminians: they do not waste time pining for absent friends for there are too many other interesting people near at hand to turn to for company. They will, however, take care to keep in touch with relatives at a distance by way of phone calls and letter-writing: Geminians spend a fortune on writing paper, stamps and phone calls.

Jealousy does not mar the friendships, love affairs or family relationships of Geminians; they can be jealous, but only of other people's intellectual gifts.

I mentioned earlier that Geminians do not need to feel emotionally secure; in fact, security of any kind is unimportant to them. For them, it represents stagnation –

and that is the one thing that your true Geminian cannot tolerate at any price. So their lives develop along episodic, disconnected lines; they certainly cover more mileage during their lifetime than many of the other types, but all too often they have little to show for it except a vast variety of experience.

Careers for Gemini? With an I.Q. above average, they are obviously fitted for occupations that require a high level of intellectual ability. Teaching appeals to them, so does anything to do with the media. Mercury was the god of Commerce, and Geminians of both sexes are in their right element as salespeople: they develop salesmanship to a fine art. Obviously, too, the kind of occupations that afford plenty of scope for change of scene, variety of stimulus, or have to do with people *en masse*, are attractive to Geminians. They are never at a loss to make an adequate income, as they can turn their hand to almost anything; but they prefer to gather earnings on a modest scale from several different sources – the kind that bring in money quickly.

Geminians of both sexes are slim, with long graceful limbs, delicate, tapering fingers, a high forehead and a 'perky' nose (rather like a pointer's, in fact); it actually twitches when they are excited. Very intelligent looking too, but attractively so, with well-chiselled features. And they are very prone to gesticulating with their hands to emphasize what they are saying. Their facial expressions are also very mobile. They are restless and fidgety: they just cannot relax completely. When thinking, they are apt to doodle with a pen or pencil, or else play with small objects. This type enjoys walking, jogging or sprinting and likes ball games, more especially tennis.

Geminians have wiry constitutions: the standard of health depends entirely on the state of their nervous system, which is a hypersensitive one. Worry can have a catastrophic effect on their health. The physical area associated with this sign is the respiratory system, which should be safeguarded that much more for this reason. Untidy in habits, Geminians are also too much inclined to be irregular in regard to mealtimes, and this can play havoc with their digestive system. They need plenty of fresh air, and this should be taken into account in regard to their places of work.

The Gemini Man

The Gemini man has a boyish air about him that is particularly appealing to women. He treats them as his equals (there is nothing of the male chauvinist pig in his character), admires them for their intelligence as much as their physical charms, and is particularly attracted to the mature type of girl and the older woman – rather than to the naïve young girl. It is important to him that his female companions are self-reliant; he adores sophistication in a woman, but takes care, if he lives in lodgings, to seek out the motherly type of landlady who will care for him as she would her own son. In fact, when it comes to man-woman relationships, Gemini has no intention of lumbering himself with a wife who is going to be very demanding, either emotionally or materially. His idea of an ideal partnership is the equal sharing of expenses, and, if possible, anything but the lion's share of other responsibilities.

A collector of trifles (both sexes of Geminians love to collect miniatures), you will notice that he carries more equipment around with him on his person than the other types. He has several pens in his breast pocket, and his other pockets are likely to be weighed down with various little gadgets which 'might come in useful', and, of course, he is never without his diary – chockful of jottings. Take a look at his little book of telephone numbers: that too is full.

The Gemini man has a boyish air that is particularly appealing to women, is a bookish man and his pockets are likely to be weighed down with various pens and gadgets.

When the Gemini man is off work, do not expect to find him spending much time at home; he is off elsewhere, making his round of calls, exchanging gossip, keeping up with what is going on in his local community. What time he does spend at home (other than when he is sleeping) will be busily occupied. He is certainly a bookish man and never begrudges spending money on books, especially the kind that adds to knowledge.

Why is it that the Gemini man marries so early? Well, it is one way of halving his expenses, and with luck his wife will help him continue his university or other college courses by handing over some of her earnings. But the chances are that she did the proposing – it helped him make up his mind to throw in his lot with her instead of one of his other girlfriends who was not so quick off the mark.

Why is a Gemini father so much an object of affection for his children? Because he joins wholeheartedly in their pleasures, though he will not let them monopolize too much of his spare time. But at least he will help with their homework.

The Gemini Woman

She makes a better sweetheart than wife – that is, if she chooses the kind of husband who expects her to devote herself entirely to the role of housewife. She is erratic in her way of handling domestic chores; and it will become expensive to her partner to provide her with all the save-time-and-labour gadgets and appliances she demands. She has no intention of spending hours preparing meals; but on the other hand she will welcome visitors to the home, and it will not bother her a bit if the place is untidy. 'You must take me as you find me' is her slogan.

The Gemini woman gets on equally well with her own sex as the opposite sex. She is always ready to give advice to friends. Very active in the local women's organizations, too, she is a great one for giving morning coffee parties.

She is very sketchy in keeping household accounts; but as, more likely than not, she too is a wage-earner, she is always ready to pull her weight with expenses.

The Gemini woman loves weekend excursions away from home (as does her male counterpart) and she insists on having her own car, as she likes to get around at top speed under her own steam. Not always the best of drivers, though: she is too easily distracted by what is of passing interest, and also apt to change lanes much too frequently, to the annoyance of other, more consistent motorists.

When it comes to choosing clothes, she loves separates and is good at teaming them together, but how she jangles! You can always hear a Gemini woman approaching – it is those items of costume jewellery she is decked with, the kind that hang loose, those chains, bangles and, needless to say, a charm bracelet weighed down with items.

The Gemini Child

The Gemini infant is a very restless baby – a very light sleeper, a baby that is quick to take notice of the world around him or her and who demands a lot of attention. Gemini children need to feel in close communication with other members of the household – so leave the bedroom door ajar when you tuck them into their cot; and leave a nightlight burning too, for they are very

The Gemini woman has no intention of spending hours cooking, is untidy, loves separates, but how she jangles!

imaginative and many feel frightened of the dark.

Teething will be a problem, and the baby will be especially fractious during this period. Once at the crawling stage, it will be well nigh impossible to keep your Gemini baby from exploring their surroundings.

This is the precocious type of child who learns to read – and to learn anything else – much earlier, and quicker, than other youngsters. And you had better provide him or her with a children's encyclopedia, otherwise you just will not be able to answer the innumerable questions fired at you, to say nothing of getting a moment's peace.

Beware when your Gemini child may seem to be absorbed in what he or she is doing while you chat away with whoever is keeping you company, as those little ears are very much on the alert. Best be very careful what you say, for sooner or later it will be repeated – and probably to the one person who should remain ignorant of what you have been saying.

At school, your Gemini child will be the delight – but also the bane – of teachers; they will praise his or her cleverness, but school reports will be full of criticism for their lack of concentration, and those other mercurial shortcomings. These children are particularly nervous at examination times, yet manage to pass with high marks, if not top marks. But care must be taken to see that they do not overtax their nervous systems in striving to excel.

As a teenager, your child will be 'into' everything that will keep him or her in the swim with companions of the same age. Creative talents will come more and more to the fore then. This type of child is, fortunately, slow to mature so far as the sex urge is concerned; so you need not worry about what will happen through constant contact with the opposite sex. In fact, throughout school life, it is preferable for the Gemini child to attend mixed schools.

When the time comes for your Gemini son or daughter to leave school, training college or university the career they embark on will be likely to get off to a most promising start. Armed with the maximum amount of A-levels or the best degrees, he or she will not have to look far for an opportunity to take on a job that will offer very bright prospects for rapid self-advancement. Indeed, Geminians are much more likely to achieve spectacular success in their careers before they are thirty years of age than any of the other zodiac groups. That is, providing they do not chop and change the nature of their work too often, for Gemini finds it so hard to stick to anything for long once it has become a matter of familiar routine. Even if Geminians do stick to their original choice of profession or business, sooner or later they will start up

The Gemini child is a precocious type of child who learns to read early.

something else and divide their time and energy between the two. This often happens when Gemini is in the early thirties or early forties.

Affinities of Gemini

Geminians are so interested in other people, irrespective of their particular zodiacal type, that they usually manage to keep on civil terms with everyone they come in contact with.

LEO (23 July–22 August). Gemini admires Leos who manage to restrain their over-restless impulses and whose warmhearted nature and generosity add to the affection Gemini feels for this type.

LIBRA (23 September–22 October). Gemini has an affinity with easy-going, affable, charming Libra: romance will be a particularly lighthearted affair between the two.

AQUARIUS (21 January–19 February). The individuality, unpredictability, and originality of the Aquarian's ideas and outlook on life fascinate Gemini.

SAGITTARIUS (23 November–22 December). There is also a close rapport between Geminians and their opposite type, Sagittarius; but Sagittarians unfortunately are apt to encourage Gemini to behave irresponsibly, and to venture far beyond his or her depth, both socially and financially.

PISCES (20 February–20 March). Gemini is very tolerant of Pisceans – as well as he may be – because Piscean shortcomings are so akin to his own: such as escaping wherever possible, from tiresome responsibilities. But Pisces turns once too often to Gemini to help him out of the predicaments his weakness has got him into – the signal for Gemini to steer clear of Pisces in future.

Geminians find it difficult to get on with the following:

CAPRICORN (23 December–20 January). They do not, however, remain long in contact with Capricornians, who are much too pragmatic for Gemini, much too limited in their range of interests and not given to the high spirits and frivolous behaviour that appeal so much to Gemini.

TAURUS (21 April–20 May). This type is a bit too placid, and much too stubborn (like Capricorn) for Gemini's liking.

ARIES (21 March–20 April) is much too bossy and his temperamental outbursts when angry shatter the poor Geminian's nerves. If forced to remain in close contact for long with Aries, Gemini will end up a nervous wreck.

SCORPIO (23 October–22 November). This type too can have a most demoralizing effect on Gemini, because Gemini knows only too well that it is impossible to hide anything from Scorpio, whose penetrating gaze quickly calls a halt to the plausible excuses Gemini thinks up on the spur of the moment to deal with awkward situations.

CANCER (21 June–22 July) is a bit too sentimental, and tearful, for Gemini and like Scorpio much too suspicious to make any close relationship a comfortable one.

VIRGO (23 August–22 September). Virgoans are much too precise, critical, and practical for Gemini: association with this type will soon give Gemini an inferiority complex, for what Geminians do in a superficial way will be revealed in all its limitations by the very thorough results produced by Virgo.

Cancer is the sign of the zodiac linked to the home and family side of life, and the Moon, its ruler, is related to motherhood. Family ties mean even more to Cancerians than they do to any other of the zodiac types, and it is particularly vital to their happiness that they feel secure in their domestic background. The Cancer girl is only too happy to learn all she can of homemaking from her mother; the Cancer male reveres his mother and he, too, does not think it beneath his dignity to lend a hand with the household chores. If reared in a happy home, Cancerians will be in no hurry to leave it; in fact, they may have to be shooed away from it when opportunities for self-advancement in their careers necessitate living far away from home. If unhappily situated in childhood, the Cancerian will make a very determined effort to build a home and family life of his or her own at the earliest opportunity. Not that Cancerians crave for a lavish domestic background; fine buildings, beautiful furniture and gracious surroundings are not important to them – they could be as contented with a house on a council estate as a Queen Anne residence in its own grounds. But, be it ever so humble, there is an atmosphere about the Cancerian's home that has an instant appeal to all who are privileged enough to be made welcome there.

However, it will not be easy for you to gain an invitation to the Cancerian's home. These people guard their domestic privacy from the inquisitive eye of strangers; even their closest neighbours are soon made to realize that proximity is no passport for dropping in on the Cancerian for a cosy chat. Do not expect a Cancer man to be willing to lend you his lawnmower or to give you any cuttings from the plants you have admired so much in his garden: Cancerians are particularly loath to part with their possessions. Be quick to accept when the Cancerian eventually asks you whether you would care to enjoy his or her hospitality – it means you are within a hair's breadth of becoming a cherished friend. Even so, you have not yet passed the final test. When you do gain admittance to the Cancerian home, you will find that you come under family inspection – and if you do not pass muster in the family's eyes your relationship with the Cancerian will make no further progress. But, if you hit it off with the family, henceforth you will be elected an honorary member of the clan – which may turn out to be a very mixed blessing, once you get to know them better!

One of the most endearing qualities of the Cancerians is the way they cherish their elderly relatives, in particular their parents. So long as Cancerians have a roof over their head, their parents can feel assured that it will be a refuge for them if ever they need it. And Cancer males feel as protective towards the other womenfolk of the family as they do towards their mothers. Woe betide the man who plays fast and loose with a girl's affections if she has a Cancer brother, father, uncle or grandfather – he will be on the warpath in no time at all. The woman who falls in love with a Cancer man must accept the fact that she will always take second place in his heart to his mother; but at least she can rest assured that the old proverb about a good son being a good husband and father will hold true.

There is a deeply religious side to the Cancerian nature, which stems from an intuitive awareness that there is more significance to life than catering for one's material requirements; and there is also a very conventional streak in the Cancerian make-up. Cancerians take their marriage vows very seriously indeed, and they prefer to make them in church or synagogue, not in a registry office.

For Cancerians, no marriage is complete until it is blessed with children. The phobias that influence so many of the other zodiac types against having more than one or two children certainly do not hold sway over this particular type. They will make sacrifices very willingly in order to give their children the best kind of education, and they will shower them with loving attention; but they do tend to become possessive. The Cancer man does not welcome the male who will take his daughter off his hands; the Cancer mother is of the firm belief that no woman is completely worthy of her son.

Cancerians are fiercely patriotic, and they are hero worshippers of any public figures they respect or who appeal to the romantic side of their nature.

Comparisons may be odious: Cancerians do not like to be reminded of their resemblances to their namesake, the crab as they are certainly apt in this case. The crab has a hard carapace that protects its soft body; Cancerians affect a tough attitude to protect themselves from succumbing too easily in situations that they feel would place them at a disadvantage. Always suspicious of, and on the defensive with strangers, they maintain an aloof manner that repels any overtures the latter make. Very shy of revealing sentimental reactions to anyone who plays on their heartstrings (unless it is someone with whom they are intimately involved, or someone their lives are closely bound up with) Cancerians adopt a very tough pose. When doing business, they also instinctively resort to tough bargaining, even though it is palpably obvious that they are being offered very fair terms.

The crab scuttles away when attacked; Cancerians also adopt evasive measures under similar conditions. If forced into a corner, the crab can use its claws to very good effect. Beware provoking your Cancerian to the point when he or she feels impelled to retaliate – they know just which is your most vulnerable spot and what they then say will leave a very deep wound in your feelings.

The crab is very tenacious. Once it grabs anything, it will hold on to it, even at the expense of losing its claws. Try to separate Cancerians from anyone or anything they value – you just cannot make them let go. The same applies to those irrational prejudices they cherish: no amount of reasoning will persuade them to discard their opinions.

Look up the meaning of the word 'crabbed' and you will find that its definition is 'cross-grained, perverse, churlish'. Cancerians can show all of these qualities when out of humour.

The Moon, ruler of this sign, is associated with inconstancy because of the changes in its phases, and Cancerian moods certainly appear to alternate with its waxing and waning. If you doubt this, then find a calendar and keep close tabs on your Cancerian at the times of new and full moon. Then you will be far less puzzled by the intensity of their emotional reactions to everyone and everything around them at those particular times.

Basically, these people are kindly, unassuming individuals; very practical, very persevering in their efforts to reach any objective they have in mind (though they often do so in a curiously roundabout way). Imagination is well developed, and they certainly possess an extrasensory faculty: never distrust the Cancerian's hunches, for ten to one they will prove accurate. And there is no doubt they can always read your thoughts and gauge your intentions.

Cancer is a 'Water' sign, and it is true that Cancerians love to be near water, on it or in it. Moonlight has a powerful effect on them too, and a very romantic one. They are nature lovers, animal lovers, and they also love variety of scene and experience – so long as neither present any danger to their basic security. True Cancerians are very ready to travel all over the world, but only if it does not mean permanently uprooting themselves from the place they call home. Though time and distance may separate the Cancerian from old friends, they will not lose complete touch with them. Cancerians take up new interests from time to time, but sooner or later they revert to those that have been pushed aside.

The best types of occupation for the Cancer-born are those trades and industries that cater to domestic requirements: anything to do with food and drink (Cancer brings the techniques of cuisine to a fine art). All aspects of farming and agriculture appeal to Cancer, including stockbreeding. Among the professional pursuits, biology and medicine are associated with this sign of the zodiac; and, of course, you will find many Cancerians in the Navy, the Merchant Marine, and the world of shipping generally.

Conservative in temperament and very much disposed to choose a secure career, Cancerians make good civil servants. It is not surprising, when you consider the importance they attach to owning their home, that they also gravitate into the building trade, and property management and development.

One of the interesting features about the Cancerian life pattern is that it is likely to unfold in seven-year cycles, of which the period around the twenty-first, twenty-eighth, and forty-ninth years usually coincide with especially important turning points in the Cancerians' personal or career history (they live to a very ripe old age).

The parts of the body associated with this sign are the chest and, in the case of women, the breasts and mammary glands; the stomach, a particularly sensitive area for Cancerians; and the ductless glands.

Physically, Cancerians have a good deal of stamina, but are particularly sensitive to changes of atmosphere, both psychic and climatic. Though those born in the northern hemisphere enter the world in summertime, Cancerians do not like to be exposed to a very hot climate; in fact, they flourish in damp surroundings. Temperature is subnormal, so the average Cancerian is not subject to blood pressure. But Cancerians are particularly vulnerable to any form of drug and should be very cautious about making use of even the mildest forms of sedatives. Alcohol is something else that should be taken very sparingly: which is unfortunate since the true Cancerian enjoys a drink. Cancerians need to watch their weight, which is also a pity because they really love good food.

The Cancer Man

A staunch upholder of the Establishment, the Cancerian male is fanatically loyal to the public figures he admires including those in the world of sport. He is very emphatic in stating his opinions and, though he will not admit it, very superstitious. He is not a rationalist, though he suffers under the delusion that his convictions are founded on logical reasoning. Like his feminine counterpart, he is entirely guided by his feelings, but, as he is very intuitive, he usually reaches the right conclusions on anything that has to do with the practical affairs of daily life.

Though he may not spend much of his working life at sea, the chances are that he has a nautical roll to his gait; and, even when completely sober, he finds it very difficult to walk along a straight line. He can be very jolly when among his closest pals, but he is also inclined to sulk rather than to rage when angry or hurt. In moments of deep distress, he may even weep – and suffer from deep embarrassment afterwards.

The Cancerian often takes on a family business, either one that he has inherited or that comes on to the market; he prefers to do this rather than risk setting up a new one. A keen fisherman, he also has green fingers and tends to take first prize at horticultural shows.

When he is in a confiding mood, he will tell you how far back he can trace his ancestors: he will have gone to infinite trouble to discover the roots and branches of his family tree. He also loves to reminisce about the good old days: in fact, he lives too much in the past and looks askance at people who fly in the face of tradition. No revolutionary, the Cancer man. Nor is he a follower of changing fashion. In fact, when forced to discard his old suits, he insists that his tailor designs new ones on the same pattern. Such jewelry as he possesses will most probably have been bequeathed to him by older male relatives. Watch the loving care with which he winds up his grandfather's watch. And once that wedding ring goes on his finger (yes, he certainly wears one) it will remain there permanently for the rest of his life – even if, by force of circumstance, he marries more than once.

The Cancer Woman

Very popular with the opposite sex because she is so very feminine, the Cancer female finds her true vocation in the role of wife and mother. She can be a bit of a flirt before she marries, but I doubt very much whether she subscribes to the ideas and behaviour pattern of today's 'permissive society': not because she is a prude, but because she knows full well that unless the partnership between man and woman is clinched by a religious ceremony the chances of it withstanding the test of time are very frail. She wants security in any relationship with the opposite sex. Moreover, she wants her children to be born in wedlock, just like her own parents and grand-parents were. She certainly would not wish to cause them any embarrassment by flouting convention.

There is often a dramatic streak in her make-up, which is why, despite the fact that she is shy, she is attracted to the world of entertainment and flourishes in it. This is the romantic side of her character seeking an outlet. Nursing appeals to her, too, and so do the social sciences. She has a very good head for business, but she will be very willing to sacrifice her career, no matter how successful it may be, in exchange for marriage and the role of housewife.

The Cancerian woman adores babies – anybody's babies – and is always willing to babysit for friends and relatives.

But oh, how moody she can be – and how tearful when unhappy! She is nobody's fool, however, and she can use tears to shrewd advantage in getting her own way with the man in her life. Although she gets on well with other women, she does not indulge much in feminine gossip. Her friends know they can trust her to respect their confidences.

She is very practical during the daytime – but what a transformation occurs when you chance upon her when she is bathed in moonlight. There is a very mysterious, ethereal quality about her then, which casts a spell over any male in her vicinity.

The Cancer woman is a great one for remembering birthdays and anniversaries. She puts great value on commemorating them, and expects the people with whom any special occasions have been shared to do like-wise. Friends, relatives and partners should bear this carefully in mind, for nothing so deeply hurts this type

The Cancer man is very superstitious, a keen fisherman, has green fingers and tends to take prizes at horticultural shows.

of woman as any indifference those near and dear to her may show to those special occasions. Married or un-married, Cancerian women are subject to recurrent fears about the loosening of the ties between them and the people whose lives are closely intertwined with their own, and instinctively seek to reinforce those bonds by sentimental gestures. If they are not reciprocated, you cannot mollify the Cancer woman by admitting that you had forgotten the significance of those dates she has underlined in her calendar: she will withdraw into her

shell and make you feel intensely uncomfortable until you have made amends for your lapse.

Cancerians of both sexes are hoarders – this stems from their thrifty instincts. Cancerian women may irritate you intensely by their constant reminders that you should not throw away anything you have no use for – 'it's bound to come in handy some day' they say as they rummage through all that junk you have selected for disposal. You may try to keep it a secret, but their mental telepathy will be on to your wavelength at these times.

34

The Cancer Child

The Cancer child is ultra-sensitive to his or her home atmosphere, and very quick to respond to the moods of parents, brothers and sisters. It is especially important that the home atmosphere should be calm and happy. If you, his parents, are at cross purposes, do not indulge in arguments in front of your little Cancerian.

A broken home can do irreparable harm to the Cancerian child's nature. This type of child seldom has much self-confidence or self-reliance, and what little he or she does possess will be badly undermined if the parents split up.

Other children are apt to accuse their Cancerian playmates of being cry-babies and to taunt them for being so dependent on the moral support of their parents. And it is true that Cancerian children are far too apt to resort to the threat that they will tell mummy or daddy if they feel they are being ill-treated by the children around them. So it is up to you to foster their ability to fend more for themselves. Beware being over-protective to this type of child.

During their period at school, your Cancer offspring will probably show a particular interest in history and geography, and they may be very musically inclined, or have a flair for painting. They are seldom outstanding in their academic achievements, though of course much depends on the individual horoscope to determine the extent of their talents. But even the most gifted Cancer children tend to be late developers, even though they usually have very good powers of memory. However, this is probably because their home life absorbs most of their interest during their formative years. If you supplement what the child is learning at school by doing some personal coaching at home, then you will discover more quickly where your child's talents lie.

Unless you have no alternative, do not send your Cancer child to boarding school – not at least until the teen years have been reached. You will achieve nothing in the way of stimulating the child's independence of spirit by taking this measure, but you will be subjecting him to unhappiness, because this type feels totally bereft if cut off for any length of time from the family unit.

Bear in mind that the early stages of puberty can be something of a traumatic experience for Cancer children, who tend to become even more sensitive and withdrawn at this time. By far the best way to explain the facts of life to the Cancer child is to provide opportunity for studying the habits of animals; if you have a farmer in the family, allow the child to be present when a foal is being delivered or a cow is giving birth to a calf. The matter of fact way in which the farmer deals with this situation will be very reassuring to the Cancer youngster.

Of course, your little Cancerian will not be an angel, but by and large these children are easy to deal with. They are inclined to tell lies when they fear the truth will get them into trouble (but so are most children for that matter) and you will have to deal firmly with this. But the fact that there will be such a particularly close bond between you and your Cancerian offspring will encourage him or her to be truthful with you, and you can then encourage the child to be equally frank with other people.

The Cancer woman finds her true vocation in the role of wife and mother; nursing appeals to her, too, and so do the social sciences.

The Cancer child will not be an angel but more than likely will be musically inclined.

to make provision for retirement and is among the best of the insurance broker's clients.

Cancer–Taurus marriage partners are especially well matched, for Taurus is the sign in which the Moon is most at home when not in its own sign.

PISCES (20 February–20 March). Cancerians tend to be protective towards their Piscean friends.

VIRGO (23 August–22 September). The Cancerian gets on well with Virgoans, appreciating their sincerity and willingness to be helpful; but he considers them too fussy and faddy about food. No true Cancerian shares the Virgoan preference for health foods and vegetarian diets.

SCORPIO (23 October–22 November). There is a bond of intuitive understanding here.

The Cancerian, in particular, has very strong likes and dislikes.

ARIES (21 March–20 April). The Cancerian's antipathy here is instinctive. Arians of both sexes are, he feels, too overbearing and rash.

GEMINI (21 May–20 June) is too volatile and too superficial to appeal to the Cancerian, even though the latter does respond to the Geminian's sense of humour.

LEO (23 July–22 August). Cancer has a sneaking admiration for Leos, but disapproves of their extravagant habits.

LIBRA (23 September–22 October). Cancer is always on guard with Librans, sensing that they can manipulate him.

SAGITTARIUS (23 November–22 December). Cancerians are too cautious to become involved in business with this type, however much they enjoy discussing politics or religion with them.

CAPRICORN (23 December–20 January). The Cancerian respects the strength of character of this type, but is repelled by Capricorn's lack of emotional warmth.

AQUARIUS (21 January–19 February). The Cancerian's intuitive insights are no help at all when it comes to understanding the erratic antics of Aquarius.

Do, however, be specially firm in insisting that these children acquire tidy habits – and do not be too sympathetic when they air their grievances about other children. This will only encourage them to harbour grudges – one of the worst failings of all Cancerians who, like the elephant, never forget and are slow to forgive. Make them well aware that forgiveness is among the greatest virtues, and that spitefulness is something of which to be deeply ashamed.

Affinities of Cancer

Cancerians seem to have a particular affinity with the following types:

TAURUS (21 April–20 May). Cancer has much in common with Taurus in a preoccupation with making money work for itself. However, Cancerians prefer sound investments to risky speculations. Every so often they will chance their luck on the latter, but only when they are doing so on a strong hunch. This type begins early

LEO 'THE LION'

Birth period 23 July–22 August

Quite a large percentage of people with aristocratic or royal blood in their veins have Leo prominent in their horoscopes; and all Sun Leos have an inborn conviction that they have a divine right to feel superior to the rest of us: even those who do not indulge in the exhibitionist type of behaviour so prevalent among this zodiac type. This regal attitude makes them very self-assured in all situations. This, and their natural capacity to take control of what is going on, and to excel themselves in whatever they organize, naturally attracts much respect from some of the other types – though Scorpio, Capricorn and Aquarius show a marked resistance to any attempt on the part of Leo to lord it over them; and, well aware that all three have strength of character equal to his own, Leos decide to ignore their behaviour. But it rankles, all the same.

However, if there is a strong autocratic strain in the Leo character, it is balanced by generosity of spirit and a very warmhearted, idealistic nature. The Leo love of power is matched by the instinct to wield it for the common good.

Many of the Leo habits are those of the domestic cat. Take heed of the instinctive behaviour of the Leo about to recline in a comfortable, well-padded and cushioned armchair. Likely as not he or she will test the cushions by kneading them before sitting down. Like the cat, Leo has a very light and slightly sinuous gait. Leo emulates the cat's nocturnal habits, and likes to go roaming after the sun goes down, even after putting in a hard day's work. They frequent the most brightly lit places where the best in food, drink and entertainment are to be had.

Though capable of titanic effort when necessity demands, Leos can also be very indolent – just like the cat. And, like the cat, they are sun worshippers (after all, the sun rules their sign) who love to bask in its rays. Like the cat, Leos are very clean in their personal habits, yet they ignore the conventional rules for keeping fit and still manage to look and feel at their best. Typical Leos are not fond of strenuous sport, nor do they stick to a regular, well-balanced diet. Instead, they gorge all those delicacies that, according to the dieticians, they should avoid, and though they put on weight they do so in the places where it is most becoming and not too noticeable. Every so often, they decide to go without a meal or two, but only because they feel like doing so. They eat at irregular times, but nothing seems to upset their digestive processes. They drink freely of good wine and liqueurs, yet neither their complexion nor their liver rebels against this. Leo believes that water is for washing, not for drinking purposes, and totally disregards its value for flushing the kidneys. When indoors, Leos shut every window tightly yet, after spending hours in rooms with the temperature of the hothouses at Kew Gardens, they will expose themselves to the most severe winter weather and still never suffer a chill. They do so only of necessity, not choice; for preference, any winter journeys will be undertaken in well-warmed vehicles.

Two other feline habits are noticeable: Leos have a very dainty way of eating their food, just like a cat; and how they scratch when annoyed, and what sharp claws they have! Leo women can be as skittish as kittens, but they are also sometimes catty in their comments about other females. When pleased, Leo voices take on a quality that reminds one of a cat's purring; their voices also take a caressive note when they are addressing people near and dear to them.

The feline strain in the Leo make-up is marked in other ways: even in appearance one is reminded of the feline signature. Leo's hair grows back from the top of the head just like the lion's mane, and the strong indentation between nose and upper lip, and the way the Leo upper lip very slightly overlays the lower, are catlike.

Leos love approbation and they will lap up flattery as greedily as a cat does cream, even though they are not deceived by it. If you want to make a good impression on Leos, just lay it on thickly and then observe them preen themselves. As an afterthought, confide in them how much you depend on them – at which point anything you ask of them will be granted.

It must be admitted that Leos do not show particularly sound judgment in their dealings with people. They believe that if you treat them right, others will respond in the same fashion, so of course they are bound to suffer disillusionment from time to time. The fact is, Leos just cannot be bothered to probe deeply into the motives of other people: they are much too self-centred. So, of course, they play right into the hands of unscrupulous people who impose on trust and good nature.

As you will have guessed by now, diffidence is not a Leo failing. No Leo hides his or her light beneath the proverbial bushel or thinks twice about facing up to anything that challenges their capabilities to the utmost. They just cannot stand criticism, so be very wary if they ask for your candid opinion about their behaviour and their talents. Even when well meant, your Leo recipient will regard an adverse opinion as a personal rebuff.

Leos radiate vitality to everyone around them just as the sun, their ruler, sends out its rays to nourish the earth. They inspire other people to give their best to what they are doing: those who come under their spell are devoted to them, completely confident that what Leos say and do is right. Loyalty is a Leo virtue, the unswerving loyalty that stands undaunted in the face of crisis. Your Leo will be especially staunch on your behalf when you are in trouble and need to be defended or rescued. Treachery is the one thing that Leos can neither forget nor forgive. Naturally religious, though not necessarily regular attenders at a place of worship, Leos have sublime faith that good will triumph over evil and that there is a power on high that will ensure that justice will prevail here on earth. High principles and high ideals come naturally to Leos; and so does a love of humanity.

According to Leo it is love that makes the world go round and they need to give and receive love in full mea-

sure in order to be at their best. Emotionally, Leos are very affectionate, protective and romantic. But they can be very possessive, too, in the sense that they feel they must come first in the affections of the other person. They do not, however, demand that those whom they love should sacrifice all other loyalties on their behalf: indeed, Leo would think much less of them for doing so. It is certainly true that, much as Leos love power, they will count it well lost for the sake of love.

Leo marriages are not always too successful, because partners sometimes feel overshadowed by the strong personality of their Leo mate; yet divorce is much less frequent among Leos than most of the other types, with the possible exception of Cancer. Leos make better parents than partners, but though indulgent to some extent towards their offspring – very indulgent, so far as material benefits are concerned – Leos demand respect from their children and take it for granted that they will be consulted before the children make any decisions of importance in regard to their careers or their marriages. Leos are not eager to marry young, and very often the women turn down several opportunities before they decide to settle down in partnership: the average age of marriage is between twenty-eight and thirty-one years of age. Very often Leos fall deeply in love again during their early forties, but even so they will not consider forsaking husband or wife.

Oddly enough, Leos are not jealous of attentions bestowed on their partner by the opposite sex; they feel too confident that he or she will not switch their affections elsewhere. After all, Leos feel so convinced that they have nothing to fear from rivals that they will boast about how much other people admire their choice of partner. Leos take rivalry as a form of flattery. It would be a great blow for the Leo to feel that others wonder what he or she could see in the person with whom they have united themselves.

Leos are not likely to have many children. One or two is the general rule, although this is not due to deliberate family planning.

Leos like to bestow gifts on others, but they do not like accepting favours. In the cruder types, pride turns to arrogance and these positively resent the efforts of people who want to help in time of need. There are other Leo traits that are to be deplored. Some Leos can become tyrannous if they meet with opposition from the people they have control over, their excuse being the ingratitude of those for whom they consider they are doing their best. Self-esteem can degenerate into blind conceit.

Leos can be a bit too ostentatious; this is the type that gilds the lily, carries pomp and circumstance to a ridiculous degree, and luxury to the point where it offends rather than appeals to or amuses other people.

Leos flourish in all trades or professions that have to do with the finer things of life. The world of fashion appeals to them and so do the arts (this is a very creative type). Many Leos go on the stage, or become performers on the cinema or television screen; others direct and produce entertainment. Goldsmiths are often Leos, for gold is the metal associated with this sign and some Leos become bullion dealers. There are also a lot of Leo pawnbrokers around. However, Leos will be found in medicine, in top-ranking positions in government departments and the diplomatic Corps, and in the Church.

Success comes fairly easy and fairly early to the Leo-born. They are well suited for self-employment, but if they decide to work for someone else they are never content till they reach the top of the ladder in whatever organization they join. If Leos go into partnerships, these are likely to go through critical phases every so often unless their associates are willing to play a passive rather than a forceful role.

Financially, Leos tend to be lucky but very rarely indeed manage to live within their incomes. They are careless and dilatory, but very honest in all monetary dealings. No use expecting Leos to keep strict account of outgoings, and when it comes to sending in income-tax returns hours of frenzied activity have to be spent sorting out all those receipts that have been stowed away at random in odd places. Very occasionally the Leo is smitten with the thrift bug, but never for long. The accumulated savings will soon be splurged on what has taken his fancy.

Physically, Leos (if true to type) have a large, round head; fine, silky hair, initially very plentiful but, in the male, thinning rapidly from early middle age; a smooth, fine-textured skin that should not be exposed for long to the sun's rays. The complexion takes on a more florid aspect in middle age, yet the skin retains its original texture. Leo eyes are prominent; the Leo gaze very direct, yet with a benevolent rather than hard look. Leos carry their heads high and walk with their shoulders held slightly backwards, so that in profile the trunk seems to slope slightly to the waistline. The upper part of the body and limbs are proportionately stronger and bulkier than the flanks and lower portions of the legs. In middle age Leos develop something of a paunch, yet it is not conspicuous because of the way they carry themselves.

Both sexes are well-dressed. In fact, as mentioned earlier, they tend to overdo it. Even the Leo male shows a great fondness for jewelry of the most expensive kind; and both sexes delight in wearing furs. The Leo actor will acquire a fur-lined overcoat as soon as he has landed a decent part in a play: before that he will probably borrow one from an opulent friend in order to impress agents. Pigskin gloves, camel-hair coats, well-cut tweeds, sharkskin evening dress, complete with frilled shirt – Leo will sport them all.

Leos are robust; their nervous organism is well balanced and they seldom suffer from neuroses. The Sun governs the heart, and Leo must be careful not to strain that vital organ of the body. Blood pressure can be another thing to guard against in later life, and hardening of the arteries. Life-expectation is higher among married Leos than those who remain celibate.

The Leo Man

He loves to do the organizing of any project, but relies on other people to deal with the pettifogging details of anything he gets going. Rather impatient by nature, he wants quick results, but will stay the course for as long as necessary if these cannot be had. The Leo male is very much in his right element in any of the armed services and his uniform will eventually be adorned with the insignia of high rank, and he will be very proud to display the medals he has won for valour.

Leo is a great man for joining clubs (like the Sagittarian).

39

LEFT *The Leo man is in his element in uniform. He will lavish chocolates and flowers on a lady he wants to please.*

RIGHT *The Leo woman, very much the central figure of her surroundings, may own a small dog and adores cats.*

He is very much a man's man, yet is always happy to have women around him – and how they adore him. He always remembers to extend those little courtesies that women appreciate so much. If he takes a lady out to dine, he will lavish chocolates on her and anything else he thinks will please. When he comes to call, he comes bearing gifts (in the plural and including flowers).

The Leo man in this country greatly admires the Royal Family, feeling that they are an extension of his own family unit. Although he means well, he can be far too condescending to those he considers his inferiors. He does not have a very well-developed sense of humour and cannot take a joke against himself. But he is very kind and this makes up for any of his shortcomings.

The Leo man does not like getting up early, which is not surprising, as he stays out so late so very often. A sophisticated man about town, he also likes to spend some time in the country and likes to play the local squire.

The Leo Woman

A dazzling creature – when arrayed in all her glory you will probably have to don dark glasses to dim the radiance that surrounds her presence. Very much the central figure of her surroundings – those bold enough to try to steal the limelight from her will be soon made to feel very inconspicuous indeed – as there is something so magnetic about the Leo personality that it rivets the attention of other people.

She has most of the characteristics of her male partner – and some of her own into the bargain; for instance, her ability to remain composed even when dealing with any crisis; and, again, her ability to remain gracious when she is dealing with boorish people.

The Leo woman collects admirers galore and puts them on full display; wherever she goes, she carries her entourage in her wake – and others will be carrying anything she needs.

She may have a small dog under her arm – very prob-

ably a peke (it is Mr no. Miss or Mrs Leo who likes large dogs). She adores cats – who treat her with the same cool appraisal that they give to other human beings. Far from resenting this, she greatly admires their dignity – and their disdain, because she respects the intelligence of the feline tribe.

No – you cannot persuade her to be photographed with lions – she is no coward but she draws the line at exposing herself to foolish risks. But you will be asked to admire the portrait of her done by the most fashionable painter of the day (actually, she will feel peeved if she has to draw your attention to it – after all it is so prominently displayed over her mantelpiece).

The Leo Child

The Leo child has many friends, and they circle round him like the planets round the sun. He is a sunny-natured child, but from infancy he shows an instinct to rule the roost, and his parents must curb this trait. Brothers and sisters wait upon little Leo, whether he is older or younger than they are.

The Leo girl takes great pride in her appearance, and loves dolls for the sake of dressing them. From a very early age she shows strength of character and very definite indications of where her talents lie; for she is a born actress and at school she will be very keen to take the leading role in any theatricals staged for parents' day.

Leo children are lazy about lessons. They put off doing homework as long as possible; they never seem to swot before examinations. Yet somehow they get through them with credit. The reason? They are never nervous at examination time, and in spite of their shortcomings it is amazing what they have learned in the classroom. After all, Leo pride could not countenance being outdone by others in the class.

The Leo girl is very strongly attracted to the opposite sex, even when very young, but little boys are apt to be less vulnerable to her charms at this stage than will be the case later. They defy her – and sometimes even poke fun at her. But not for long: when aroused, she resembles the tigress rather than her namesake.

Affinities of Leo

The people with whom Leo get on best of all are those born at these times of the year:

ARIES (21 March–20 April)
SAGITTARIUS (23 November–22 December)

As all three types belong to the same 'Fire-element' zodiac-group, they share certain characteristics in common – namely, self-assurance, powerful feelings which express themselves in exuberant behaviour – all three have a burning desire to live life to the full; all three are courageous, always ready to face up to life's challenges. There will be rivalry between them at times, but it will be friendly rivalry which stimulates them to show their capabilities to the full. When things are going well, Leos are apt to become lazy and 'rest on their laurels' but association with Arians or Sagittarians

The Leo child shows an instinct to rule the roost from an early age and brothers and sisters wait upon little Leo.

impels them to overcome this failing in order to keep well abreast with what Aries or Sagittarius are accomplishing. Aries benefits from association with Leo because the latter is able to persuade Aries from being too foolhardy. There's only one danger which has to be avoided when Leos become closely involved with Sagittarius – that is, each encourages the other to live beyond their means because they both share the same love of luxury.

Leos are also attracted to people born at these times of the year:

GEMINI (21 May–20 June)
LIBRA (23 September–22 October)

In this case, it is because Gemini and Libra stimulate the imagination of Leo – and help Leo to take a more objective view of people and situations at those times when they are too much under the sway of their emotional reactions to both.

There's another bond between Leo and Libra – both are artistic, and the impeccable taste of Libra is something which Leo admires (and emulates).

AQUARIANS (21 January–19 February) are the 'opposite type' to Leo – which is why they are often disposed to link up in partnership – but, if the partership is to be a success each must be willing to make allowances for the basic differences in their natures. Leo can be thrown off balance by the dispassionate attitude of Aquarius – the impartial way in which they handle their relationships; Aquarius may be irked at times by Leo's very conventional outlook and behaviour. Aquarians are determined to be a law unto themselves, and Leo must accept this and resist the urge to try to bring influence to bear on an Aquarian partner.

People with whom Leo may find it that much more difficult to remain on amicable terms are those born at these times of the year:

TAURUS (21 April–20 May)
VIRGO (23 August–22 September)
CAPRICORN (23 December–20 January)

These are the 'Earthy' types, whose outlook on life may be too pragmatic, too materialistic, for Leo's liking. Taurus and Capricorn are too 'stodgy' for Leo, too limited in their interests; Taurus becomes jealous of Leo's popularity, and this produces strain in their relationship. Capricorn is far too unemotional for Leo, who is abashed by the cool way in which Capricorn responds to Leo's affectionate overtures. Moreover, Capricorn's failure to be impressed by the success of Leo affronts the latter. In Capricorn, Leo recognizes a force that is that much stronger, that much more effective, than his own. As for Virgos, they tend to be much too critical, and much too fussy to suit Leo, who is exasperated by their anxiety complex – and their thrifty habits.

The other types with whom Leo runs into difficulties are those born at these times of the year:

CANCER (21 June–22 July)
SCORPIO (23 October–22 November)
PISCES (20 February–20 March)

The moodiness, reticence and excessive sensitivity of these 'Water' people are characteristics which make it impossible for Leo to judge their reactions – Leo just doesn't know how to handle them at those times when their behaviour seems most mystifying.

VIRGO 'THE VIRGIN'

Birth period 23 August–22 September

Virgoans are very praiseworthy people, as I am sure you will agree if you have much to do with them. They are admired for their strong moral principles and the fact that they really do live up to their maxim of 'do as you would be done by'. They are respected for their humanitarian qualities, the fact that they really care about what goes on in the world, and that they are prepared to do what they can to alleviate suffering and to further the cause of justice. Then, again, how delightful it is to be able to have a really intelligent discussion with them, without getting into a heated argument, about matters on which your points of view differ. And they never cause you embarrassment in mixed company by unmannerly behaviour.

But to be frank, Virgoans can be a bit of a trial at times. You may be feeling in the mood to enjoy a spell of quiet relaxation, but can you do so when in their company? Not unless you have superhuman, mesmeric powers that you can bring to bear on them. For Virgoans cannot relax of their own free will: they have to keep busy, it is an obsession with them, and they will see to it that they keep you on the go as well. Although they do it with the best of intentions, there are also times when they offer unsolicited advice you feel you could well do without, for it is the kind that is tinged with criticism.

In fact, it is the Virgoan's hypercritical attitude that most exasperates their associates. Very rarely indeed do they give unqualified praise. For if there is a flaw in anything, Virgo will be quick to spot it; but it should also be stated that the type is equally quick to suggest what should be done to correct it. You must admit that though the Virgoan you have in mind is a fault-finder *par excellence*, he or she always offers constructive criticism. All the same, it has to be acknowledged that Virgoans merit the accusation of being hair-splitters – they do quibble over trifles.

All this is only to be expected, however, for Virgo is the sign of perfectionism. This is one explanation of the symbol of the sign: the overflowing cornucopia in the arms of the virgin represents the time when the seed brings forth Nature's perfect offering to Man – the full fruits of harvest.

As for the virgin herself, she represents chastity rather than virginity. She represents chastity in thought as well as in behaviour. It is true that, by and large, Virgoans are pure-minded: they do not instinctively believe the worst of anyone; they are offended rather than amused by crude jests. In fact, there is often a quality of innocence about the true Virgo that should not be misinterpreted as ignorance.

It is also true that some Virgoans can become 'hung up' on sex. They are not included among the highly sexed zodiac types. At best, their attitude to sex is they can take it or leave it – they certainly do not suffer the frustrations experienced by their more sensual brethren if forced to lead a celibate existence. They certainly do not flaunt their sexual conquests in order to arouse envy in those less successful – though they could have good reason to, for they are certainly in great demand for their favours. Both men and women Virgoans have sex-appeal. They may or may not be particularly attractive physically, but there is a certain something about them that especially appeals to the opposite sex. It is that air of fastidiousness, and that wholesome quality they possess. Whoever is attracted to Virgo is not thinking of having a casual affair: he or she wants to settle down with a Virgo partner, the ultimate compliment that can be paid from one sex to the other. However, Virgoans are in no hurry to marry; more often than not they are too bound up with their career, no matter what it may be.

This is an 'Earth' sign, ruled by Mercury. Virgoans are very practical, very industrious, extremely conscientious about their work, and very methodical in the way they go about it. They are also walking encyclopedias, for if they have a hobby it is always a useful one, and what is more useful than gathering knowledge? And they do so very thoroughly too; unlike Geminians (the other type that has Mercury for its planetary ruler), Virgoans have the patience and perseverance thoroughly to master anything that attracts their attention. Like Gemini, Virgoans will quiz you mercilessly when they become interested in you or in what you are telling them – and how exasperating it can be to deal with their recurrent interruptions when you are eager to get to the climax of your account. But at least you have their undivided attention. And what long memories they have! Their only rivals are the Taureans and Scorpios. When you have upset them, how Virgoans harp on old grievances, tagging them on to fresh ones. And how they nag at you to do what you have promised, to remind you of anything you have been shelving. When you remonstrate with them they protest plaintively that it is for your own good. Life shared with Virgo can be a bit tough at times.

Virgo is the sign of service, and Virgoans are quite happy to fulfil the role of employee. In fact, they more often than not choose it even when they have the opportunity to be self-employed. This is because Virgoans lack self-confidence and underrate their capabilities. If called upon to exercise authority, they prefer to do so on equal terms with other associates rather than to take full responsibility. They need to feel they have moral, and physical, backing. They do not try to evade responsibility – but they certainly welcome the protection that carrying out other people's orders gives them.

In addition to that inferiority complex, they also have an anxiety complex about the future. Faith and optimism come in short supply to them; they cross their bridges long before they reach them, and fear the worst rather than hope for the best. Like the other two 'Earth' types, Taurus and Capricorn, Virgoans are hell-bent on providing for their future security. It explains their thrifty habits, the caution they exercise before reaching important decisions; they will let opportunities for self-advancement pass by if they feel at all doubtful about their capacity to measure up to what those opportunities involve. That is, unless they have somebody behind them to give them a nudge forward. Otherwise, if they are doing reasonably well, they are not likely to exercise much initiative to do better.

The best careers for Virgoans are those that give full outlet to their intellectual scope, their preference for analytical work, their ability to stick to routine – and their humane instinct. All forms of public service are right for Virgoans; they are natural bureaucrats. A large proportion gravitate into occupations to do with social welfare, education, health and hygiene (and, in particular, mental health: Virgo is often prominent in the horoscopes of psychaitrists and psychologists).

If Virgoans turn to the arts, literature and journalism may well be their choice of profession (they combine both); editors, art critics, writers on specialized subjects are very often Virgoans. But they are also to be found in profusion in the various branches of science. Alternatively, those who have a special talent for delicate manual work become dentists, or jewellers or makers of precision tools. Other than that, they prefer office work to factory work, even if they gravitate into industry.

Virgoans have a very delicate nervous constitution, and it plays havoc with their digestive system. This type is more prone to a grumbling appendix than the other zodiac types. They are much preoccupied with the business of keeping fit, for Virgo is also the sign of health and hygiene. It is a rare specimen who does not take great care to keep in good trim by maintaining abstemious habits and taking plenty of exercise (as if they did not get enough with all the flitting about from place to place). Very clean, they are also very neat in their appearance; even after a long stint of manual work, they manage to preserve a fresh, tidy appearance.

Physically, Virgoans are well-proportioned though rarely above average height, of slim build (not so much because they are careful of their diet but because the acidity in their system keeps strict control of the fatty tissues). Like Gemini, Virgo has beautifully shaped hands and feet, slim limbs, large, soulful eyes; and, like Gemini, they retain something of youthfulness in their appearance even well past middle age. But there is a subtle difference between the Geminian and the Virgoan in this respect. There is a much more serious, thoughtful aspect to the Virgo face – those worry lines that crisscross their foreheads do not make Virgoans look older, but they do draw attention to the nervous disposition of the type.

Virgoans make good parents; they take a keen interest in their children's education, and make the work of teachers easier by doing some coaching. They bring discipline to bear on their offspring in a reasonable way, for the Virgo parent is no tyrant and treats the child on the same basis as an adult, and is always prepared to explain patiently why this or that should be done. Moreover, Virgoans set their children a very good example in the way of correct behaviour, tidy habits, and consideration for others.

The Virgo Man

A bit fussy and faddy, perhaps, but the sort of person that other men refer to as a 'thoroughly decent chap'. The Virgoan man would be willing to share a night out with the boys, but really prefers more intellectual forms

of entertainment than a stag party, a tour of the pubs or clubs that his friends may consider an essential form of amusement. He listens politely to their racy conversation, but does not contribute to it, though he will talk his head off on politics or any other serious topic. If the jokes become too blue, or if anyone on the scene shows signs of becoming belligerent under the influence of drink, Virgo will find an excuse to take his leave. He has no intention of witnessing or taking part in brawls.

The Virgo man becomes a member of the kind of clubs and societies that exist for laudable purposes. He likes to travel; the chances are that he also likes sightseeing, and makes a point of taking full advantage of the museums and perhaps the art galleries accessible to him. He puts very great store on culture. He can be a little bit of a snob – but an intellectual snob rather than a social one.

He has a place for everything, and gets very irritable if he finds that whoever does his cleaning for him does not return his possessions to their right places. He cannot concentrate on anything he is doing if he is surrounded by any kind of muddle. Virgo man cannot always see the wood for the trees – he becomes much too preoccupied with the minor details of projects.

Virgo is anything but a show-off. In company he is content to let others steal the limelight. His cool, aloof manner when among strangers is in fact due to shyness; but he can soon be drawn out. He is a very adaptable man, although from choice he prefers to stick to familiar ways. But his commonsense accepts the necessity for change if progress is to be maintained, and he will be ready to lend support to any experiments that he considers to be based on sound reasoning.

If Virgo man does take a dislike to anything or anyone, he holds fast to his opinion, for this, too, is the product of rational judgment, not emotional bias.

He is hospitable, but does not attempt to impress others by making lavish gestures. He takes good care to get to know his prospective partner well before he plunges into

The Virgo man has intellectual leanings, likes political discussion, and travel and puts great store on culture.

marriage – that is, if he does not decide to remain a bachelor. Unfortunately, the middle-aged Virgo bachelor develops very old-maidish ways, which increase as he grows older. Never one to shirk his responsibilities, Virgo does not really condone the 'permissive society'. Nevertheless, if he feels he has met the right partner, the fact that he is tied down to an unfortunate marriage, or that she is, will not prevent him from undergoing the trials and tribulations that accompany divorce or, if divorce is out of the question, of setting up house (discreetly of course) with the woman concerned. And he will take pains to prove that he intends to be faithful to her. One thing he will not do is shirk his obligations to his ex-partner – or break up someone else's happy marriage. If he flouts the conventions, he does so only of necessity, and not for selfish reasons.

women (like their male counterparts) do tend to be hypochondriacs; leave Virgoans to browse through a medical dictionary and the next thing you know they will be rushing off to their doctor for yet another thorough medical check-up. Though very sensitive to pain, they are brave when it comes to facing the dentist, for they have a horror of losing their teeth through neglect.

She is not a prude, but on the other hand the Virgo woman does not really enjoy sex, no matter how deeply devoted she is to her mate – unless of course there are other factors in her individual horoscope to stimulate her sexual appetite. For this reason, if her marriage is otherwise satisfactory, she will not take it too seriously if her partner finds sexual consolation elsewhere; she certainly will not ask for divorce merely on the grounds of his adultery. Even if she has a passionate side to her nature, she does not rate sex sufficiently important to make a fuss about it. Like many Latin women, she accepts the fact that one has to allow for the difference in sexual attitudes of the male and female, and, so long as he is discreet about his little affairs, she is prepared to turn a blind eye to them.

The Virgo woman presents an immaculate appearance, her home is perfectly run, she is a hypochondriac, and will not take it too seriously if her partner finds sexual consolation elsewhere.

The Virgo Woman

You will not catch a Virgo woman with her hair in curlers, or slopping around the house in a dressing gown; from the moment she leaves her bedroom first thing in the morning (and she is an early riser) to the moment she retires for the night, she presents an immaculate appearance. She has very good taste in matters of dress and make-up; knows full well that it is a mistake to follow fashion slavishly; spends much less on her clothes than most of the other types (but that is because she usually sticks to classic styles that are never outdated). She seems to have a special penchant for antique jewellery – and she likes to have pewter ornaments around her, too.

Her home is perfectly run, and she is a very careful housekeeper who keeps strict account of what she spends and never gets into debt. There will always be sufficient on the table to satisfy everyone's hunger at meal times, but she calculates weights and measures very meticulously so that nothing will be left to go to waste.

Her home will be adequately furnished, but not overcrowded with furniture; it is not very colourful, either, for Virgo women are very restrained in their choice of colours, and often have a preference for neutral shades of furnishings. Take a peep into her medicine cupboard; it is likely to be crammed with bottles of pills and medicine, and a very well-stocked first-aid kit. For Virgo

Love is not blind, though, in other respects, so far as Virgoans of both sexes are concerned. Loyal though they are to their nearest and dearest, they are very clear-sighted about the shortcomings of relatives, partner and close friends – and not at all slow to remind them of these.

The Virgo Child

The Virgoan child is very much a credit to his or her parents, and receives good reports from school, and at parent-teacher meetings parents will glow with pride when they are complimented about the child's excellent manners.

Even while still very small, the outstanding characteristics of the type are evident in little Virgoans. These children manage to remain clean when others around them look very begrimed, and they certainly care for their clothes. Do not make the mistake of buying a garment on the off chance that your son or daughter will approve of your choice – they want to do the choosing themselves. When the time comes to pass on the things they have grown out of, these will be in very good condition. Virgoans cherish their toys – there is nothing destructive in the Virgoan nature, even if the little Virgoan is as critical as the older generation born under this sign. Which is why it pays to take notice of what young Virgoans have to say when they choose to comment on what you are wearing or what you are doing: they have old heads on young shoulders and their advice will be very shrewd.

You can always make Virgo children happy by giving them books to read and instructional toys, and they like to make things. If your little Virgo daughter expresses a desire to learn carpentry, do not fob her off with the comment that it is a more suitable hobby for boys. Later on, you are going to be grateful for her ability to turn out some very fine cabinet-work.

Though shy, Virgoan children are gregarious and therefore make an effort to get on friendly terms with schoolmates. Other children tease them for being 'goody-goodies' and 'teacher's pets' but, all the same they turn to the Virgoans for advice, and behave all the better when in their company. Do not worry unduly if you have to send your Virgo child to boarding school; Virgoans do not cling to the family as much as Cancerians, and are able to adapt themselves to the change of environment far more easily than might be supposed. Eventually, they will reach the status of prefect; they never abuse this, for there is nothing of the bully in the Virgo child or adolescent.

They love to collect things, especially stamps, coins and whatever else has an educational (to say nothing of financial) value. They are more likely to spend their pocket money on items of lasting value than on sweets or other ephemeral pleasures.

Virgoan children undergo traumas when examination times draw near. Their anxiety is at peak then but, despite their nervous tension when the ordeal has to be faced, they come through very credibly, as their retentive memory comes to their aid.

Young Virgoans are very fidgety (like Geminians), but you never have to find an answer to a plaintive plea of 'What can I do next?' for your Virgo child always finds plenty to do.

Take pains to foster the child's self-confidence. Never much in evidence, it collapses all too easily when this child is outshone by other youngsters. At such times the best course is to point out that while another may be very clever in some ways, your little Virgoan has the advantage over them in other directions.

Encourage your Virgoan child to be more emotionally demonstrative by making it clear that it is never embarrassing to show affection in other ways than by merely doing one's best to be useful. Let Virgoan children keep pets: you need never fear that they will be careless in looking after them. Do not be surprised, however, if they show a greater fondness for dogs, rabbits and mice than for cats. A lot of Virgo children have a cat phobia.

One important piece of advice: see to it that your young Virgoan does not become the prey of other children's bossy, selfish attitudes; these children can be too easily imposed upon because they are so ready to be obliging.

The Virgo child of either sex likes to make things and shows a greater fondness for dogs, rabbits and mice than for cats.

You can safely send your Virgoan adolescent to a co-educational school, for though they form platonic friendships with the opposite sex in their teens (it helps them to mix all the more easily with them in early adult life), there is little danger that your teenager will want to experiment with sex at an early age. These children are very late developers in that respect. Your child's main aim will be to get through college or university with good results, and nothing will divert him or her from that purpose.

Affinities of Virgo

The Virgoan particularly likes the company of individuals of four zodiac types: TAURUS (21 April–20 May), CANCER (21 June–22 July), LIBRA (23 September–22 October) and CAPRICORN (23 December–20 January).

AQUARIUS (21 January–19 February). With this type the Virgoan maintains an amiable relationship: both have the same coolness of emotion. The Virgoan does not always agree with the very advanced ideas and unconventional quirks of the Aquarian. He respects them, however, because he is aware that they reflect the Aquarian's strong convictions.

SAGITTARIUS (23 November–22 December). Virgo admires this type for its keen sense of justice and its breadth of vision – but is horrified by Sagittarian extravagance.

PISCES (20 February–20 March). Virgoans feel particularly sorry for Pisceans and will exercise a lot of patience in trying to help them sort out their troubles. In the end, however, will be forced to admit that it is hopeless trying to bolster the Piscean's willpower. The Virgoan gets on much less well with some of the other types:

ARIES (21 March–20 April). Virgo is apt to disconcert Arians by criticizing them and questioning their ability. Virgo's attitude to LEO (23 July–22 August) is similar, and the latter's extravagance shocks Virgo.

GEMINI (21 May–20 June). Virgo takes Gemini to task for his exaggerations – and for untruths, which Virgo cannot tolerate at any price.

LIBRA 'THE BALANCE'

Birth period 23 September–22 October

Librans give the impression of being nice people with nice manners for charm is a basic ingredient in their make-up. It is not an affectation: it comes naturally to people born under this sign to be courteous, friendly and obliging, to do all in their power to maintain harmony between themselves and their associates. For Venus is the planetary ruler of Libra, and Venus is the planet of peace and love.

Librans are never happier than when they are matchmaking. So beware if you are revelling in your state of single blessedness, for your Libran friend or relative just cannot believe that this is the case, and assumes you are just making the best of a bad job. There is a very strong motive behind all those invitations you are getting. Have you not noticed how the conversation always seems to turn towards marriage and its advantages, and that, among any other company present, there is always an unattached member of the opposite sex? No use trying to make it clear to Librans that you have no intention of getting hitched – it will not discourage them from their purpose, which they will probably achieve unless you move out of reach.

Librans have a marvellous flair for manipulating people and circumstances; that is why they are in such demand as mediators, arbitrators, negotiators and ambassadors.

Poise is another outstanding characteristic in Librans, which is linked to the fact that the Balance is their sign. Inwardly, they may be feeling out of their element in their surroundings, but they will not appear to be ill at ease, for they are adept at 'carrying off' any situation. Even their movements are particularly graceful, and that is why you find so many professional dancers are Sun Librans – and, of course, this sign is usually well to the fore in the horoscopes of trapeze artists. They can be thrown wholly off balance by anything that takes them completely by surprise, particularly if it is disconcerting. Only at such times are they likely to go to extremes of behaviour – but not for very long.

Librans are essentially good-natured, considerate, easy-going, and of mild disposition. They are motivated by the urge to get the best out of life by adapting themselves to, rather than trying to create, the conditions around them; and it works out well for them too as they seem to achieve their aims with much less difficulty than the other zodiac types. They do not try to bulldoze their way through obstacles, but manage to find a way round them. Libra is one of the 'communicative' signs, and Librans like to be in close communication with the world around them. Because they are so ready to identify themselves with the aims of others, they are naturally suited for partnerships and, indeed, can only feel completely self-fulfilled when living and working in harmonious partnership with others. Pacifists by nature, nonetheless if forced into a position where they are left with no alternative than to fight, Librans can be very formidable opponents, not by resorting to brute strength but

by resorting to strategy: they bring it to such a fine art that it is their most powerful weapon of defence. There is another aspect to the Libran's nature that will become increasingly obvious to anyone who keeps them under close observation. When Librans feel a sense of grievance against people with whom they are involved, they will not make an open display of it, but they are expert at stirring up trouble for them by the most subtle means. For they can as skilfully set people at odds with each other as they can unite them, while seeming to be totally blameless.

There is much more than meets the eye to charming Libra, and this should be borne in mind by those who imagine them to be very harmless, very inoffensive and totally free of any impulse for mischief-making.

The symbol of the scales is a reminder that there is a very cool, calculating brain functioning behind the bland expression and disarming manners of Librans. They are perpetually preoccupied with making comparisons in order to distinguish relative values. It is this attitude of mind that enables Librans to see things from other people's point of view, for they look at everything from all angles. 'If I were in your position, I'd feel the same' says the Libran when appealed to for reassurance by anyone who is in doubt about, or who wants confirmation of, his own judgment. If Librans feel compelled to criticize or censure the behaviour of others, they will manage to do so without arousing resentment on the part of the people concerned; they are able to make it easier for people to swallow what is unpalatable by sugaring the pill of criticism with the coating of tact. Diplomacy is part and parcel of the Libran's nature.

Librans believe in moderation in all things and, by sticking to the middle course, they avoid the pitfalls that bring down people prone to carry excess to dangerous lengths. Idealistic in outlook, Librans never blind themselves to the realities of life that make it necessary to temper idealism with practical commonsense. Librans do not become over-ambitious, over-enthusiastic, over-optimistic – or unduly pessimistic. Though pleasure-loving, they do not carry the inclination to enjoy themselves to the point where it exceeds all other inclinations. They do have some ambition, but at the same time are conscious of their own limitations.

This temperate attitude shows itself in their close relationships. Venus is the planet of love, and life would be meaningless for Librans if they had inadequate outlets for their affectionate, and romantic, inclinations. Happiness means much more to Librans than wealth or fame, and in order to safeguard happiness in personal relationships they adapt themselves instinctively to the needs of friends and loved ones. They make no attempt to monopolize the time or attention of partners, relatives or friends; similarly, because they cannot centre their interest or affection on any one particular person, they will firmly but tactfully fend off any attempt on the part of their close associates to make undue demands on them.

47

Theirs is a give-and-take attitude; and, bearing in mind the symbol of their Sun sign, remember Librans will never be prepared to accept short measure in return for what they give.

It is instructive as well as amusing to observe the tactics of Librans when they are bargaining; it is likely to be a prolonged operation, for this type will be very persistent – their aim being to wear down the resistance of whoever they wish to come to terms with. Librans employ 'soft sell' rather than 'hard sell' tactics – they never adopt a 'take it or leave it' attitude. Quite the reverse, for it appears that they are very willing to make concessions, and to effect a compromise. But those who believe that they are getting the better of any deal with Librans are deluding themselves. Be wary of accepting favours from Librans, and do not feel conscience-stricken when they seem to be making sacrifices on your behalf – for you may be sure that there will be strings attached, and that sooner or later you will feel the tug of them.

Librans have a well-developed aesthetic sense and are very responsive to beauty in any form. More often than not the Libran possesses some kind of artistic talent, more especially for the visual arts. Artists and designers come under this sign, for in matters of colour and form, few are more talented than the Libran. Refinement is the keynote of all that Librans create, and refinement is the keynote of their tastes, manners and habits.

Since Venus is the ruler of this sign, it is not surprising that Librans of both sexes are among the more physically attractive of the zodiac types. Libran women may not have perfect physical proportions, but they come very near to the ideal dimensions, at least in youth; in middle age they have to take extra care to avoid putting on too much weight.

Symmetry is a particularly marked characteristic of the Libran physique; there is a well-balanced look about the Libran face and body and, again, a certain refinement about the physical hallmarks of Libra. A round head, rounded forehead of average height, an oval face, dimples in the cheeks and chin, well-set, very expressive eyes which often appear larger than they are, a chiselled nose, a beautifully shaped mouth, small ears, small, even teeth (usually very white), a slim supple neck, well-shaped hands, limbs long in proportion to trunk. Both hair and skin are of fine texture. The only defects are the ankles and feet; the former may be rather thick, the latter rather stubby.

Men and women alike born under this sign have excellent taste in dress and in what they surround themselves with in their homes (though they spend most of their time elsewhere, for domesticity has no exaggerated appeal for them). They are very sociable, and though they appreciate the beauties of Nature, they prefer to spend most of their time in town where there is an abundant variety of sophisticated entertainment, rather than in country pleasures. You certainly will not find them following the hounds, or taking part in a shoot, for Librans consider blood sports cruel and abhor all cruelty.

Libran failings? They have an instinct for taking the line of least resistance to avoid discomfort of any kind and a rather fickle attitude to romance (after all, Librans are always seeking the ideal partner, so you really cannot blame them if they try out one after another). They can also be fair-weather friends: do not expect to see much of them when things are going badly for you and people are ganging up against you. Librans will make themselves scarce then, as they do not want to jeopardize their own popularity and well-being if either would be put at stake by coming to your aid.

The main failing of this type, however, is vacillation at times when resoluteness is called for. This indecision is only natural for the Libran who so carefully weighs up the pros and cons and finds that they happen to be in balance when the matter demands a decision. This being one of the 'Air' signs, there is also a restlessness in the Libran nature that makes these people lose interest in anything that becomes too familiar, too much a matter of routine. Librans crave plenty of variety.

Another failing is a tendency to become too dependent on other people because they are poorly endowed with self-confidence. However, over the last ten years or so, Librans have been showing more self-reliance and independence. This is because Uranus moved through their sign between 1969–1974, and Pluto moved into it in 1974. But Pluto will leave Libra late in 1983, so the chances are that Librans will revert to their normal habit of taking their lead from others.

So long as they stick to their usual policy of moderation in all things, Librans enjoy good health. Like the rest of the zodiac types, they have their particularly vulnerable bodily areas and organs; Libra 'rules' the lumbar region of the body, and any kind of nervous or emotional stress will react on the kidneys – and, in consequence, cause Librans to suffer from very acute headaches, amounting to migraine. They are particularly sensitive to their environment, and health will suffer if they are forced to live or work in depressing surroundings, or where they are exposed to too much tumult. It may also be added that Librans have an acute distaste for involving themselves in the more unpleasant or the very arduous kinds of work. They prefer the office to the factory floor; the lighter kinds of jobs to those involving heavy manual labour; the glamorous rather than the more prosaic occupations.

The Libran Man

A perfect gentleman, sophisticated and witty, with polished manners, he is very much the man-about-town. He dresses well without being over-ostentatious in appearance and mixes well in company without trying to dominate the scene. He is very popular with the opposite sex because he really appreciates their company; he gets on equally well with his own sex, but other men take care to mind their p's and q's in his presence. He does not make it obvious that he does not like crude behaviour, but the fact that he himself does not indulge in swearing, and makes no attempt to match the 'blue' jokes of male companions with any of his own, has an effect on them. He can be a bit of a disappointment to the full-blooded female who expects him to be a passionate lover; for though he adores flirtation and indulges in romantic gestures, sex itself is not all that important to the Libran man. Maybe the fact that he is not over-keen on strenuous physical exercise accounts for his not being the most exciting bedmate.

Other men envy him his good looks, though they may affect to scorn them because he is the matinee idol type.

They also envy him the apparent ease with which he seems to make headway in his career; yet he is not likely to arouse any real animosity among them. They consider him to be a bit weak, a bit too much of a ladies' man.

He is at his best when acting on behalf of others. A marvellous salesman and troubleshooter, he is the one who is called upon to settle disputes between management and labour, though more often than not you will find him representing management rather than the trade union.

The Libran man is the 'perfect gentleman', a marvellous salesman and mediator in disputes. He enjoys a gamble.

As a husband, he is very willing to leave the decisions to his wife. As a parent, he shirks the task of reading the riot act to children when they misbehave – so it is no use his wife trying to bring them to order with the threat of letting their father deal with them. The youngsters know full well that their father is a pushover, and that the most he will resort to in the way of disciplinary action is to have a heart-to-heart talk with them.

Libran man is prone to fits of laziness, and there is a streak of the gambler in him because he cannot resist the temptation of trying to make money the easy way. He is not too prompt in paying his bills, and all too willing to obtain on credit terms luxuries that he cannot afford to pay for straight away. However, he does not allow himself to carry this weakness too far – an example of his moderation in all things.

The Libran Woman

She is much tougher than her male counterpart, though she manages to disguise the fact. Expert at handling the mere male, she convinces him that he is pleasing himself and that she is the most submissive of mates, when all the time she is twisting him round her little finger.

The Libran woman knows how to make the best of her appearance on very little outlay – but that is partly because she is clever with her needle. She creates a delightful home, again without going to great expense. Others remark how peaceful the atmosphere is there, for she creates harmony around her. She is not an enthusiastic housewife though; if she had the means she much prefers to get someone in to do the cleaning. She can be very untidy (like Libran man). Do not expect her to be punctual.

The Libran woman is expert at handling the mere male and knows how to look her best on very little outlay.

But she is always ready to welcome visitors, not objecting when her husband brings them home without advance notice, and you can be sure she will not be caught out looking far from at her best. In fact, her husband's one grumble is that she takes far too long to get herself ready to go anywhere; in trying to decide what to wear she is likely to try on everything in her wardrobe.

A Libran woman is an affectionate but not very possessive mother. Her children are encouraged to be self-reliant and to mix freely with other youngsters. But she does have a weakness for believing that all her geese are swans, much to the irritation of other mothers when she insists on the point.

The Libran woman is a great asset to her husband because he knows he can rely on her to help him in his career. She will go out of her way to be the perfect hostess when he brings his associates or superiors home. She will also take trouble to form social connections of her own that can be of benefit to him.

She has, however, one particular weakness. Like her male counterpart, she cannot resist indulging in flirtations, though she has no intention of being unfaithful to her husband. For all Librans are very susceptible to the opposite sex, and they receive so much flattering attention from them that they are not to be blamed for exploiting it to reinforce their inadequate self-confidence.

The Libran Child

Young Librans are very impressionable, and because of this care must be exercised in the kind of children they mix with. They easily come under the influence of their companions and also become much too attached to them. In other respects, though, Libran children are easy to handle, and a delight to parents and teachers. Their desire to please, plus the fact that these youngsters are by nature amiable and well-mannered, not given to over-boisterous behaviour and not inclined to become self-willed, or too venturesome, means that they give those who have them in their care very little cause for worry.

But Libran children must be encouraged to persevere with their studies, and also to develop tidy habits and punctual ways.

It will be very hard to avoid being over-indulgent with them: they cast that magic spell of charm over everyone right from the cradle.

The main problem that those who have the care of Libran children have to face is that the Libran child is lacking in self-reliance; and therefore must be encouraged to think and act for himself or herself instead of constantly appealing for support from others. Thus, they must be given responsibilities and made to face up to them resolutely. Bearing in mind that the strongest urge in Librans is to get through life with as little difficulty as possible those who are their parents and teachers must be on the alert for the Libra child's tactics for extricating themselves from awkward situations – their tendency to shift the blame for their misdemeanours on to others.

Affinities of Libra

Librans generally mix easily with the other zodiac types.
AQUARIUS (21 January–19 February). Libra is in sympathy with the Aquarian's advanced ideas and humanitarian ideals.

The Libran child is amicable and well-mannered and casts a magic spell of charm over everyone right from the cradle.

PISCES (20 February–20 March). It may seem curious that there is a special bond between Librans and Pisceans, but Librans are able to enter the dream world of the Pisceans, towards whom they are most indulgent.
GEMINI (21 May–20 June). Librans relish the company of people of this lively, amusing type.
LEO (23 July–22 August). The warmhearted nature of Leo is thoroughly appreciated by Librans, who do not at all resent this type's love of the limelight.
SAGITTARIUS (23 November–22 December). Sagittarians are liked because they reinforce the Libran optimism.
Librans make it their business to be civil even to those people with whom they feel no affinity:
ARIES (21 March–20 April). Librans generally look askance at the brusque manners and tactless ways of this type.
CANCER (21 June–22 July). The moodiness, suspicion and timidity of Cancerians may be irksome to Librans.
CAPRICORN (23 December–20 January). Too much of the company of earthy, phlegmatic Capricorn can cast a shadow over Librans.

SCORPIO 'THE SCORPION'

Birth period 23 October–22 November

Scorpio has two symbols and it is tough luck on people born under this sign that the one commonly used is the venomous arachnid and not the noble eagle. The ancient astrologers intended these symbols to indicate the very powerful forces for good and evil within the Scorpio nature, which account for the struggle that goes on within the Scorpio individual. Hitherto, writers of astrological textbooks have all too often overstressed the faults of Scorpios and made scant, if any, reference to their praiseworthy attributes. Only relatively recently have astrologers been making amends for the prejudices and exaggerations of their predecessors.

Even so, it must be admitted (and none will be more willing to be honest about this than Scorpios themselves) that people born under this sign do have some very undesirable traits that have to be brought under control, and eventually 'outgrown'.

Intensity is the keynote of the Scorpio character; this is a 'fixed' sign and it is also of the 'Water' element. Scorpios are intensely emotional people, hypersensitive in their reactions to everyone and everything around them. Intuition is very highly developed in this type; add to this the fact that Scorpios have a very analytical type of mind, very strong will power, and an iron determination to succeed in whatever they do and you will realize that these are people who have to be reckoned with.

Fortunately Scorpios are also very self-disciplined: this is Nature's way of providing them with a self-defence mechanism they can bring into play when they choose to repress their baser instincts. And, to do them justice, they certainly try to live up to the best in their nature; it is just that, at times, their trials and tribulations get the better of them and then they yield to the temptation to 'get back' at life for dealing harshly with them.

You will gain a fuller understanding of the Scorpio nature by considering the implications of the symbols of the sign. There are various species of scorpion, and some have a much less venomous sting than others; some do only temporary and minor harm to their victims rather than kill them. Though the natural habitat of scorpions is a hot or tropical country, they are so sensitive to heat they easily die if exposed for long to the sun's rays, and must keep under cover as much as possible, if not beneath stones or in rock crevices, then by burrowing into the ground. Scorpions are 'loners' who avoid each other unless engaged in combat or the act of mating (and unless the male makes a swift getaway after the mating act he is liable to be attacked and devoured by his mate).

Scorpios can be secretive, like their namesake, but what they keep under cover they do so because of their sensitivity to other people's reactions. They take pains to hide their feelings for fear of being thought weak or foolish for displaying them, and this makes it difficult for them to be demonstrative about their affections. It is only when they become very angry that their self-restraint breaks down, and the result can be as cata-strophic for them as for the people against whom their wrath is directed. Yet it is what Scorpios say rather than do that leaves the object of their attack in a state of collapse. The Scorpios' sting is in its tail, and what Scorpio says when angry cannot easily be forgiven or forgotten.

Scorpios are 'loners' by instinct, not because they are naturally unsociable but, since they arouse such powerful reactions in other people for no good reason, they are forced to be on the defensive. Scorpios can, figuratively, kill the love that others feel for them by becoming too possessive towards partners, family and friends. For when they do become involved with anyone, they become very deeply involved indeed; and the need to feel emotionally secure in such relationships leads them to be much too demanding. They find it very hard to reconcile themselves to the fact that they cannot entirely monopolize the affection others have to give.

However, the other symbol of this sign is the eagle, the high-soaring monarch of the air who builds his eyrie in a tree-top or on a rock pinnacle, and this reminds us that, when Scorpio overcomes his mental and emotional handicaps, he (and, of course, she) can surpass all other zodiac types in saintliness. For there is a spiritual side to the Scorpio nature, and when this is activated people born under this sign become utterly selfless in their devotion to the people they love or the cause they serve.

Though they have strong personal magnetism, Scorpios do not make ostentatious use of it; there is nothing of the exhibitionist in a typical Scorpio as there is in a Leo or an Aries individual. Yet, even if they remain unobtrusively in the background, others are always conscious of their presence. Very often you will find that these people are 'the power behind the throne', and quite willing to allow others to take the credit for what they achieve. For Scorpios do not put much value on public recognition of their talents; for them, it is sufficient to know that they have achieved perfection in what they set out to do, and that they will so continue. In fact, to others it seems that they often take too great pains to bring what they are doing to the highest standard. 'If a job's worth doing it's worth doing well' and 'Hard work never killed anyone' are favourite remarks of Scorpios when others comment on the amount of effort they make.

Careers for Scorpios? Obviously those that enable them to make the best use of a high degree of intelligence plus a capacity for hard work. They excel in scientific and academic occupations, and anything of an investigatory nature (if they go into the police force, they gravitate into the CID). In the medical world they become outstanding as psychiatrists or psychologists. In the field of commerce they become consultants, experts in helping others to sort out their business problems. And, of course, because they have such powerful emotions, many also have outstanding dramatic talents that bring them fame in the theatre. This is not the only branch of the arts in which they excel: many gifted writers, painters, musicians, composers, and sculptors have the sun in this sign or Scorpio prominent in their horoscope. Whatever medium is chosen to express their gifts, the signature of Scorpio will be impressed upon it by the deep insights into the matter concerned. Scorpios may be secretive by nature, yet their work reveals much that has previously been obscure, misunderstood, or that people have hitherto been oblivious of.

One must not forget, either, that people born under this sign very often have a religious vocation, which enables them to sublimate their basic instincts. These are the people who become missionaries as well as mystics.

Scorpio is the sign of the zodiac most associated with sex; and it is true that most Scorpios have a very powerful sex drive. However, do not take this to mean that Scorpio is promiscuous. To Scorpio, the sex act is much more than a physical act: it is a symbol of a complete spiritual and mental as well as physical affinity between two people of different gender. Scorpio has a reverential attitude to it for this reason. That is why Scorpios suffer so deeply if they discover that their partner has been unfaithful; the relationship is irrevocably damaged, for they cannot forget, even if they manage to forgive, this act of betrayal.

Scorpio is very dutiful towards the family (like Capricorn), although more often than not relationships with the rest of the family are anything but harmonious. Nonetheless, Scorpio will rally round when relatives are in trouble. And how staunch Scorpios prove when their friends are in trouble; this is one of the most estimable qualities of the people born under this sign. So is the courage with which they will stand by their convictions; it matters not at all to them if this means going against public opinion.

One of the other good qualities of people born under this sign is that, though they form very powerful likes and dislikes, they can be objective about the people with whom they are not in affinity. Even if they cannot 'take to' the person concerned, they will respect his or her good qualities. This is one of the ways in which the conflict between mind and feeling shows itself in Scorpios.

Scorpios have a strong physical constitution, but it can be undermined by self-indulgence. This is the sign that 'rules' the generative organs and the eliminatory organs. Scorpios are therefore prone to problems relating to kidneys, bladder, bowels and the sex organs. They are also subject to minor throat problems (this is because there is a 'reflex action' between opposite signs, and Taurus, the sign opposite to Scorpio, rules the throat).

One of the odd coincidences noticeable among Scorpios is that so many of them suffer injury to the nose: it is not surprising if someone breaks the Scorpio nose, as the type can be so provocative on occasion when being obstinate, over-critical, jealous (and jealousy goes to the extreme in this type). Quite often in these days of cosmetic surgery, however, Scorpio decides to change the shape of its nose (it is seldom one of the best features of this type).

In appearance, the outstanding feature of Scorpios is their penetrating gaze. It seems to bore into you and it has a hypnotic effect. Scorpios are not deliberately trying to mesmerize you – it is just that they are giving you the benefit of their undivided attention, which should be flattering to you. More often than not, though, it makes the person under observation acutely uncomfortable. The Scorpio body is quite slender in youth, but shows a more sturdy aspect in middle and later life. The eyes appear to be deep set because the ridge of the bone above the eyes is more prominent than in other types (except Aries and Capricorn).

Some outstandingly handsome people are born under this sign; it is not, however, a sign that is associated with feminine beauty – Scorpio women are very attractive, but they usually have strong rather than delicate features. Both men and women have a very distinctive gait – to those walking behind them it seems as though they are swinging an invisible tail!

The Scorpio Man

He is very sagacious in business matters; thrifty without being mean in handling finances; subtle in tactics when playing the power game – yet he will not take advantage of anyone weaker than himself. He is bound to be a bit of a puzzle to you at times because you cannot fathom his thoughts. Scorpio can be relied on to keep his promises – and if he does indulge in threats, you can be sure he will carry them out. Do not try to imitate him by doing likewise, as he will call your bluff. It is unwise to hold a pistol at the Scorpio head, as he would rather die than yield to pressure of any kind.

Scorpio man is definitely at his best on the field of battle and the skill he shows in handling edged tools

The Scorpio man is thrifty but not mean in handling finances and is in his element in sport.

The Scorpio woman certainly has 'it', in fact she has the reputation of being a femme fatale.

(as surgeons, for instance) and weapons is due to Mars' rulership of this sign, though he is not a warmonger by choice. He is also very much in his element in sport, which appeals to his love of a challenge and is a harmless way of expressing his combative impulses.

He is wonderful as a lover, but his partner will find him very exacting as a husband; and he can be tough with the children, too, even though he is immensely proud of them and will make great sacrifices in order to give them a good start in life. But there is no question of who is boss in the Scorpio man's household, even though he does not fly off the handle as quickly or as frequently as Aries. It is those ominous silences of his that make everyone else at home sit up and take notice.

Scorpio man does well in the world, and deserves every ounce of success he gets, as he relies solely on his own merits, not on influence to gain what he aims for.

He likes to travel, and chooses the more sophisticated spots to relax in when he is on holiday. He likes the sophisticated pleasures of the town, too; Scorpio is a gourmet when it comes to food and his taste in wines is incomparable.

The Scorpio Woman

There was a time, some thirty to forty years ago, when sex appeal was known as 'it'. The Scorpio woman certainly has 'it'. In fact, she has the reputation of being a

femme fatale, and other women envy her ability to cast a spell over the male. But Scorpio women do not try to steal the affections of their friends' husbands or lovers, and they are not to be blamed if they figure in triangular romantic situations. These seem to be forced upon them, largely because the man they choose to wed tries in time to escape their clutches – and is only too happy if another male will take his place! He even goes so far as to warn his competitor of what he is letting himself in for.

Scorpio women are careerists by nature rather than housewives; so the way to keep a marriage on an even keel, if you happen to marry a Scorpio woman, is to encourage her to use her drive and energy elsewhere than at home. That will make her easier to live with; do not ever delude yourself that you will be able to keep anything secret from her. And it is useless trying to fob her off with lies: she knows when you are thinking of telling untruths, and she will forestall you by telling you what you intended to say.

As a mother, she is devoted to her sons but may become jealous of her daughters when they reach the nubile stage. She cannot help resenting the attention they get from the opposite sex when she is around.

Life with a Scorpio woman will be very stormy at times, but it will also be very rewarding for husbands and children who take the trouble to understand her type, and who are tactful enough to overlook her foibles. She

55

has the capacity to inject vitality into everything and everyone around her, and she will be a most stimulating influence when things are not going well for you.

The Scorpio Child

The Scorpio child is a sensitive child who needs very tactful, but firm handling during the formative years. First and foremost, this child must be especially encouraged to mix with other children – preferably those of very strong personality who will be able to stand up to Scorpio. Likewise, as this child needs to cultivate the ability to share what he or she has with others, and parents must be very firm in insisting that toys are not held on to for too long, but passed on to others who may be in need of them. Scorpio children are very keen on pets, and this enables them to show the protective side of their nature. But they are children who can be very violent when angry, and care must be taken to bring their temper under control.

As they grow into adolescence, they will become more and more self-controlled, but also more and more secretive; and parents must learn not to pry unduly into what they are thinking or doing. Scorpio children deeply resent this intrusion into their privacy. Left alone, they will not do anything to be ashamed of, but if provoked into rebellion because parents become too suspicious, they will deliberately do things that will be frowned upon. (They, too, are very suspicious, and uncannily discerning about the relationships between their parents. So, if your marriage is not very happy, you will have to be especially discreet in keeping this fact from a Scorpio child.) They need to feel emotionally secure in their home life – a broken home can do much to ruin the Scorpio character.

At school, Scorpio children will do you and themselves credit; but do not prolong their education beyond the stage absolutely necessary for a good grounding for a career. The sooner these children get to grips with the world at large the better. They will make their way ahead all the more surely for having to fend for themselves earlier than other children.

Affinities of Scorpio

As mentioned earlier, Scorpios have difficulty in handling their personal relationships, so friendships, romance and marriage are rather turbulent. However, there are certain zodiac types that Scorpio is much in affinity with, and with whom they have happy and lasting relationships:

TAURUS (21 April–20 May), VIRGO (23 August–22 September) and CAPRICORN (23 December–20 January). These 'Earth' types are so stable and so consistent that Scorpio feels safe in any relationship with them.

CANCER (21 June– 22 July) and PISCES (20 February–20 March). Scorpio also feels safe with these two 'Water' types, with whom there is an intuitive bond of sympathy and understanding. Cancer and Pisces look to Scorpio for strength and are quite willing to submit to the emotional demands Scorpios make upon them.

Scorpios have difficulties with some of the other zodiac types:

ARIES (21 March–20 April), LEO (23 July–22 August) and SAGITTARIUS (23 November–22 December). These 'Fire' types are the ones with whom Scorpios are likely to clash – it is a case of a conflict of strong personalities.

GEMINI (21 May–20 June), LIBRA (23 September–22 October) and AQUARIUS (21 January–19 February). Scorpios have an ambivalent attitude to these 'Air' types. From an intellectual point of view, they are attracted to these people because they have imagination and are stimulating companions if Scorpios are in the mood for discussion and debate. On the other hand, the fact that these three types are not very deep emotionally creates a barrier.

The Scorpio child needs to cultivate the ability to share what he or she has with others and parents must insist that toys are not held on to for too long. He can be very violent when angry.

SAGITTARIUS 'THE ARCHER'

Birth period 23 November–22 December

Sagittarians are gamblers in the broadest sense of the term. Not only are they a godsend to turf accountants, owners of casinos and dog tracks, football pools and lottery promoters, but they are always prepared to run risks to fulfil their career ambitions, their romantic inclinations and, above all, to give full outlet to their adventurous and explorative impulses. Jupiter, the planet of providential protection, is ruler of this sign, and other zodiac types are apt to be envious because Sagittarians seem to attract more than their fair share of good luck.

The Sagittarian outlook on life has a good deal to do with the way things work out for people born under this sign. Not only are they blessed with boundless faith and optimism, but they are also endowed with foresight and this gives them their sense of right timing for what others might consider their most foolhardy ventures. Breadth of vision enables them to gauge the full potential of opportunities that come their way, and they never miss them by taking too long to make up their minds. Impulsiveness stems from their love of action; their drive carries them ahead at top speed.

Sagittarius is a dual sign, and Sagittarians express their duality in various ways. They may seem to be very happy-go-lucky, pleasure-loving and self-indulgent, yet there is nothing superficial about their mentality. Your Sagittarian may be something of a playboy (or playgirl) but is also greatly attracted to intellectual pursuits. It is possible for Sagittarians to be very sophisticated in outlook without losing their religious beliefs. Sagittarians see no reason to become ascetics in order to preserve their faith – unlike some other types their religion gives them great enjoyment rather than pangs of conscience. The Sagittarian might become a scientist, but no one born under this sign could be an atheist. Deep down in the Sagittarian there is an intuitive awareness that there is more meaning and purpose to life than can ever be explained in scientific terms, and that man is destined for immortality. At the same time, Sagittarians see no virtue in turning their backs on the means man has provided himself with for getting as much fun, as much comfort and as much excitement as possible out of his worldly environment.

Sagittarians have a particular predilection for the rituals that man has devised for expressing his religious beliefs. They are much attracted to pomp and panoply in general, and even though they will at times be very casual in the way they dress, they always wear what is correct for any special occasions. And how they look forward to those official functions that provide opportunity for wearing uniforms (with decorations, of course), elegant evening dress, gorgeous ball gowns. And after watching the antics of the Sagittarians on the dance floor you will probably come to the conclusion that they would do better to stick to outdoor sports. They may be in their element if the band strikes up the mazurka or the polka – then they can prance around to their heart's content –

but otherwise they seem to find it impossible to glide in graceful rhythm to the orchestra. Should the musicians strike up 'The Galloping Major', woe betide any unfortunates in the path of onrushing Sagittarians.

It is ironic that Sagittarians, who are so humane, so benevolent in other respects, are so keen on blood sports. Shooting and hunting (though maybe not fishing, for that requires patience, and the Sagittarian has very little) have an irresistible appeal for people born under this sign, the women as well as the men. In fact, they excel at most sports, and are renowned for their sportsmanship. You will not catch Sagittarians making an exhibition of themselves because they have lost in competitive sport; they smile bravely, say all the correct things to the winner and, on such occasions, bear themselves with great dignity. This is because Sagittarians put great value on appearances – in this they are very conventional. However, when occasion permits they will kick over the traces – but they manage to do so discreetly, so discreetly that society turns a blind eye to their peccadilloes. Sagittarians too put on blinkers when it suits them to be blind to what they do not wish to see or accept.

Hypocrites? Well, this charge has been levelled at them, so maybe there is a grain of truth in it. It is certainly true that these people find convenient ways of getting out of predicaments. A Sagittarian man may be a sugar daddy to some gorgeous blonde, but he is not prepared to declare this openly to the world at large – so he passes her off as his ward, or his secretary.

As a matter of fact, the male Sagittarian remains a fancy-free bachelor at heart. He can fall passionately in love, but he does so much too often. Sagittarians in societies where more than one wife is allowed may have legitimate scope for their romantic inclinations. Otherwise, the Sagittarian man who marries may have to face up to divorce if his mate takes his romantic adventures too seriously. She will be a fool if she does: in other ways he is one of the best of spouses, being very open-handed when it comes to spending money, very ready to entertain her friends and relatives, and never a nuisance about the house – for he spends most of his time away from it, if not at work, then at the club, the pub (not because he is an alcoholic, but he loves the camaraderie of male companionship), the racecourse or the sports ground. And what a marvellous host and raconteur he is.

Sagittarians can be very temperamental and they are certainly highly strung, like thoroughbred horses. There is a lot that is 'horsy' about the typical Sagittarian, who shies at anything that disconcerts him or her, who is quick to bridle if anyone does anything offensive. Another horsy mannerism is the Sagittarian laugh. It may not resemble the untuneful bray of a donkey, but there is a whinnying note to it. And the Sagittarian male does snort to express his scepticism about anything he does not believe.

The old saying that you can lead a horse to water but

Capricorn

VS

Sagittarius

SAGITTARIUS

cannot make him drink is certainly true of the average Sagittarian. These people are open to gentle persuasion and very susceptible to flattery, but try dictating to them and their reaction will be one of very stubborn resistance.

Physically, too, you can trace certain equine resemblances. They are long-limbed like the horse, with the same high-bridged long nose and full mouth of very large teeth (the two front teeth often have a gap between them); young Sagittarians remind you of mettlesome colts. There is a tilt to the corners of the Sagittarian eyes – very bright eyes, with a twinkle in them when they are in a good humour and about to pull your leg. For Sagittarians do take the mickey out of you – but they do it in such a good-humoured, amusing way that it is difficult to be annoyed. There is something noble about

Sagittarians value their freedom above everything else: they cannot be fenced in, and those who are linked with them must bear this in mind. For this reason, they are best suited to occupations that allow them plenty of scope for handling things their own way, allowing them to move freely in varied surroundings. They have a special flair for the legal profession, and you will also find many of them among the dignitaries of the Church (Sagittarius might become a roving missionary, but he will not remain for long a humble cleric in a poor parish). Most Sagittarians reach the peak positions in whatever profession they take up. In the world of commerce, they become bankers or presidents of large organizations. If they turn to professional sport, they are apt to become champions and record breakers.

The Sagittarian man loves the wide open spaces and, if he can afford it, big game hunting.

the Sagittarian forehead; it is high and wide, the forehead of a philosopher (or at least the popular conception of one). Loose-limbed and of high-stepping gait, Sagittarians have long, narrow feet and long, narrow hands.

Sagittarius is the sign of the zodiac that physically and physiologically is associated with the hips, thighs, liver and arteries. Sagittarians are all the healthier for being fond of outdoor life and keen on exercise. But they have to curb their love of food if they are to avoid putting on too much weight. The Sagittarian male prides himself on being a gourmet and connoisseur of wines, but liverish upsets may be the penalty for these interests.

If Sagittarians seem to be accident-prone it is only because they delight in running physical risks. The sports in which they are apt to indulge are usually the more dangerous ones; but their luck holds good in that they are more likely to be injured than killed in any accident.

The Sagittarian places much value on maintaining good relationships with family and in-laws. This is not difficult, given his genial nature and generosity.

There is a strong likelihood that the Sagittarian will switch careers at least once; alternatively, the type will sooner or later take up a secondary career and maybe even a third one. The number 3 plays an important part in the life history of Sagittarians; and the thirtieth year of life is usually an important turning point for good in their fortunes. In youth somewhat reckless, in middle age always very respected pillars of society who uphold the Establishment even if they do not agree with all its rules, Sagittarians are hearty, wholesome members of the human race.

The Sagittarius Man

He is very much at home in the boardroom, where he usually sits at the head of the table; he is equally at home in the country, where he assumes the role of squire to the

The Sagittarian woman likes to read every romantic novel she can. Although she loves animals, she will hunt them.

manor born, even if he has no hereditary claims. He looks equally good in city suits, top hat and tails, and in tweeds. A gentleman by nature, and a *bon viveur* by choice. He has his failings, of course; he can be inconsistent, capricious, much too restless and, where the opposite sex is concerned, rather fickle. He usually has two love affairs going at the same time, which puts him in a dilemma when a choice has to be made between them.

If you get the better of him, he will not think less of you. When things are not looking too rosy for him he never loses heart, but, like Mr Micawber, waits in hopeful expectancy that something will turn up to change the situation. His sixth sense quickly tells him when that is about to happen. Like Leo, he never lives within his means, yet always seems to have the wherewithal to settle his debts (honour forbids that he should try to wriggle out of them). Without making any obvious attempt to do so, he collects around him friends who are better off financially, or more influential than himself, and they propel him forward. He never forgets a kindness and repays it handsomely.

The Sagittarian man works in spasms, but has lazy fits, too. He blows hot and cold by turns in his attitude towards whoever and whatever he becomes involved with. He moves house frequently or, if affluent, runs several homes in different areas (one of which may well be an idyllic love nest).

He is proud of his wife and never denies her anything – except his undivided attention. As a parent he is equally indulgent to his children, but he cannot be bothered to take a close interest in what they are doing. However, the Sagittarian man is the type who thinks carefully about his son's education long before the boy is old enough to attend it. He loves the wide open spaces and, if he can afford it, big game hunting; he suffers from claustrophobia in very confined surroundings. The Sagittarian man may be found in the Royal enclosure at race meetings; but the jockey and stable boy, to say nothing of the lasses involved in this sport of kings, will also have Sagittarius prominent in their individual horoscopes. So has the racing tout.

Sagittarius is very much a man's man, for all that he is so popular with the ladies. He is always something of an aristocrat, be his background ever so humble; very, very occasionally he is bit of a bore, but only when he is a little too pompous, a little too self-complacent. But then, who is perfect?

The Sagittarius Woman

She looks a lady, even if she is a bit of a tomboy at heart; she wears twin sets and pearls to perfection, and also looks her best in sports clothes. Very leggy, she is the envy of her dumpier female associates. The Sagittarian woman is a scatty housewife, but an enthusiastic organizer of fêtes and Women's Institute functions. From youth onwards, she attends church regularly (earlier on, it is partly because she has fallen in love with the curate); she often marries someone of the cloth. She is more than a bit of a flirt, but is never prone to heartache as she can fall in and out of love so easily. Not that she is unfaithful to her husband (in this she differs from her male counterpart), but she does console herself when marriage settles into a dull routine by reading every romantic novel she can lay her hands on. Like Sagittarius man, she loves animals as much as she loves the people near and dear to her, but she, too, will hunt them and does not shrink from seeing animals killed.

The Sagittarian woman can seem very disdainful when she looks down her long nose at you: you had better find out quickly what you have done that does not measure up to her standard of behaviour. But she will share all she has with you if you are in trouble, even if you are not in her good books at the time. She takes pains to disguise the fact, but is something of a blue stocking with a very wide knowledge of different subjects. No one expects a woman to be logical, and Sagittarian women are no exception to the rule; yet their judgment on all important matters will be very sound.

She expects her children to do her credit, but does not nag them to excel themselves – her confidence in their abilities does the trick and encourages them to test themselves to the full. She is always ready and willing to entertain their friends, but she may not always be at hand when her children need her advice – she is too busy with whatever she is organizing for her neighbours. The Sagittarian woman runs a happy, but not a well-regulated home. When she goes shopping, she always buys in bulk; much goes to waste in the Sagittarian household because of this.

The Sagittarian Child

A roamer, right from the time he or she starts to crawl; very eager to explore new ground, very quick to adapt to new surroundings. The Sagittarian child may decide to run away from home, not because he or she is unhappy there, but solely for the sake of the experience. However, you can sidetrack this impulse by encouraging your young Sagittarian to go camping with other youngsters. Boarding school has no terrors for this child, who is not dependent on the emotional security of the family background and who never has to be coaxed to go to stay with elderly relatives who live at a distance – the change of scene compensates for any inconveniences.

Truthful by nature, your Sagittarian youngster will be quick to own up to any misdemeanours; and you have not the heart to punish him or her for them, as usually no harm was meant. These are such high-spirited, energetic youngsters that they must have plenty of outlets for their driving force.

True, at school Sagittarian children may seem to be much more keen on sport and the social aspects of school life than on mastering what they are being taught; yet they do well in examinations, for their intelligence is high and they can learn very quickly. Eventually, they will become monitors or prefects, but this never undermines their popularity with fellow pupils, for they handle authority in a very affable way. Trust the Sagittarian to deal effectively with any school bully – not so much by force, as by ridicule, much to the delight of youngsters who have been terrorized.

You will have to be firm about doling out pocket money, though; and equally firm with friends and relatives who are willing to supply what you deny. I have pointed out earlier in this character sketch that Sagittarians are lucky in money matters: it always seems to come their way from one source or another. You will also have to teach

The Sagittarian child is a roamer and luckily money always seems to come their way.

your Sagittarian child to be tidy and methodical, otherwise the rooms he uses will look as though they have been hit by a tornado.

These youngsters fly away from the parental nest very early in life – as soon as they can afford to have their own pad, they will be on the move. It may cost you considerable effort to keep track of their whereabouts after that, as they do not stay put for long (like Geminians). The chances are they will go abroad at the earliest opportunity – and they do even better abroad than at home. You will have no need to worry about your Sagittarian child's future: these youngsters never turn out to be failures. Their exploits may make your hair stand on end at times, but you will be proud to brag about them.

One thing to be careful about in dealing with Sagittarian children is not to overdo discipline yourself, or to subject them to strict disciplinarians. For Sagittarians cannot tolerate undue pressure put on them. Friendly and accommodating by nature, they will respond fully to tactful ways of keeping them under control; but if they do become rebellious no amount of punishment will have any good effect. Quite the reverse; courage will then become bravado. These children have a strong sense of honour, and if this is appealed to they will never do anything to stain it. Exact a promise from a Sagittarian and it will be kept – for though those born under this sign can be inconsistent, they will never break their word: it is their bond. This, and their ambition to excel in all they do, will take care of any problems that arise during their formative years. But they can be very careless as well as over-generous with their possessions, and are apt to lose them or part with them too easily to other children. So you must see they are not imposed on by covetous companions.

Affinities of Sagittarius

Being of a generous disposition, Sagittarians are naturally disposed to be friendly towards people with whom they come in contact, although of course they find this easier with some types than with others. They have much in common with the two other zodiac types of their own 'Fire' group:

ARIES (21 March–20 April). The link between Sagittarians and Arians is their mutual impetuosity and love of adventure, and the fact that both set out deliberately to add excitement to their way of life.

LEO (23 July–22 August). The Sagittarians' affinity with Leos is based on their mutual love of luxury, their romantic attitude of life, their joint respect for conventions and love of pomp and circumstance, and the fact that they are 'lucky' to each other.

Sagittarians also get on especially well with the 'Air' zodiac group:

GEMINI (21 May–20 June). The link here is the love of both types for variety of scene, contact and interest: Gemini and Sagittarius make excellent travelling companions. As each appreciates the other's sense of humour, this adds sparkle to the relationship.

LIBRA (23 September–22 October). Tolerance and a love of fair play are the qualities Libra and Sagittarius share. The fact the Libran greatly admires Sagittarius boosts the latter's morale.

AQUARIUS (21 January–19 February). Relationships between Sagittarians and Aquarians are cordial because neither type attempts to bring influence to bear on the other, each sharing the compulsion to remain a free spirit. There is a difference between them in the Sagittarian's instinctively conventional attitude and the Aquarian's nonconformist outlook, but the 'live and let live' policy of both prevents this from driving a wedge between them.

Of the 'Water' types, Sagittarius is most at ease with PISCES (20 February–20 March); after all, Jupiter is part-ruler of that sign. There is a spiritual bond between them as both have strong religious inclinations and both take an active part in the charitable organizations that come under the control of the Church. There is another strong link between these two types: their love of a good time. They are apt to encourage each other in self-indulgent escapades, much to the annoyance of relatives who deplore their irresponsible behaviour on such occasions.

Earth and Fire do not mix well. The 'Earth' types are apt to put a damper on Sagittarian spirits:

TAURUS (21 April–20 May) likes to move at a steady pace which makes Sagittarius, galloping ahead, very impatient. The Taurean also has a too limited, too materialistic outlook for the Sagittarian.

VIRGO (23 August–22 September) is too cool, and analytical, too fussy and faddy for Sagittarius. The thriftiness, sedateness, and the anxiety complex of the type also irk the Sagittarian.

CAPRICORN (23 December–20 January). Capricorn's pessimism and sometimes very narrow-minded outlook and lack of emotional response to warmhearted, extrovert Sagittarius are characteristics that make any strong bond between the two types impossible.

CAPRICORN 'THE GOAT'

Birth period 23 December–20 January

Capricornians are tough; they need to be, for life can be harder for them than it is for the other zodiac types – they seem to be singled out for more hardships and deprivations. Saturn is the planetary ruler of this sign – the planet known to astrologers as 'the hard taskmaster' – and people with Saturn powerfully placed in their individual horoscopes are likely to be called upon to shoulder heavy responsibilities that force them to make some personal sacrifices, whether of money, freedom, happiness or comfort. Queen Elizabeth II was born when Capricorn was on the eastern horizon of the sky (as seen from her birthplace) and Saturn was dominant in the heavens. She had to take on the burden of monarchy when only a young woman; notwithstanding all the privileges attached to her position, she has been chained to duty in the service of the peoples of the United Kingdom and the Commonwealth.

Although Saturn may be 'the hard taskmaster' he equips those under his authority with the necessary character traits to meet his exacting demands: self-discipline, stamina, consistency, resourcefulness and, above all, self-reliance. Capricornians, if true to type, have all these qualities and, the sign being an 'Earth' one, they also have a very realistic, practical outlook on life. They do not take refuge in a dream world to escape from the harsh facts of life; they plan methodically in order to achieve their aims in life and they hold fast to those plans, no matter what obstacles are placed in their path.

This is the sign of the goat, and astrologers are fond of pointing out the goat-like characteristics of the Sun Capricornian. Like that hardy little animal, Capricornians can endure privation: indeed, they make a virtue of it. For there is an ascetic streak in the average Capricornian; he or she is not dependent as the other types are on creature comforts or luxuries and can be content with making do on little. You will not find true Capricornians indulging in wild bouts of extravagance once they have become prosperous. No matter if they start out with nothing and have to toil hard and long to amass money, Capricornians do become very prosperous eventually; they will restrict themselves to the barest necessities in order to put something by and they never risk their savings on speculative ventures; they stick to the sound 'lock up' type of investment.

Astrologers emphasize the difference between the domesticated goat and the wild mountain variety that manages to elude capture by leaping nimbly from crag to crag, judging distance with uncanny accuracy and retaining a sure foothold in even the most precarious places. The inference is that those Capricornians who have no scope for furthering their own aims will stoically accept the conditions imposed upon them, while those given the opportunity to make their way ahead in life will not only do so with iron determination, but also without making the wrong moves or mistiming the right ones. Ambition is one of the outstanding traits of Capricornians, and they pursue it with singleness of purpose.

Capricornians are, indeed, careerists who will not allow sentiment to interfere with their worldly aims. They love power because power will also give them full scope for self-reliance as well as bring them the respect they crave from other people. Authority means more to Capricorns than wealth; it gives them the utmost satisfaction to be able to take command of any situation.

Extremely conscientious about all they have to do, Capricornians demand the highest degree of efficiency from those who come under their authority. Tolerance is not a trait usually noticeable in typical Capricornians, and those under them who try to make excuses for their shortcomings will get short shrift. But, if not easy-going, they are certainly very just in their dealings with others. They may not bestow fulsome praise on those who please them, but they will show their appreciation in practical ways, and see that the person who deserves promotion and a rise in salary gets it. Another estimable quality of Capricornians is that they are very loyal to the people who have any claims upon them and will always help and support them in times of adversity.

When it comes to family relationships, Capricornians will make supreme sacrifices on behalf of relatives who depend on them. Where there are several children in a family, ten to one it will be the Capricorn son or daughter who takes care of the parents when brothers and sisters go their separate ways. Many a Capricornian elderly spinster has turned down opportunities for marriage for this reason.

If true to type, Capricornians cannot be described as lighthearted, high-spirited people (those who possess these qualities have other factors in their horoscopes to thank for them). As a rule, Capricornians are very serious, sedate people, and pessimists rather than optimists. This is their way of safeguarding themselves against disappointments. Even when things seem to be going well for them, Capricornians keep their fingers crossed and prepare themselves for the worst: which can be extremely aggravating to associates who are urging them to take advantage of their circumstances to ease up on work, get more fun out of life, and spend more on creature comforts.

Just as in youth Capricornians seem much more mature in behaviour than others of their own age, so too they may look older than they are; but the ageing process is slowed down once they reach their thirties: they 'wear' well in middle and later life, partly because they are not prone to excesses of any kind.

Although, with Longfellow, Capricornians subscribe to the conviction that 'Life is real! Life is earnest!' that does not mean they do not get any pleasure out of it. Pleasure, to Capricorn, means the satisfaction of knowing that you have done your duty, that you are making full use of your capabilities to practical purpose. That is why even their hobbies are not pursued for enjoyment alone but generally have some sensible purpose; frivolities have little or no appeal for them.

Capricorn

Aquar

Capricorn

CAPRICORN

It might be supposed that, being so serious in temperament, they lack a sense of humour. This is not so: in fact a sense of humour is another of the safeguards with which they protect themselves against the buffetings of fate. But it is certainly not a jovial sense of humour; it takes on a satirical quality.

Capricornians are deep thinkers rather than eloquent conversationalists; in fact, they are as sparing of words as they are economical in other ways. But what Capricornians say is always very much to the point – and they can be very blunt when asked to express their opinions. Compliments have no effect on this type: you will not be able to flatter your way into their confidence.

The goat's eye may not be its most attractive feature, but it is a very shrewd eye. Their deepset eyes look out upon the world with a cool, calculating gaze. Make no mistake – Capricorn can read you like a book; in no time at all he or she has taken your measure. Mentally, too, the Capricornian can gauge distances (remember the little mountain goat, who escapes death and injury by never miscalculating his leaps) and other measurements in his mind's eye. Ask a Capricorn housewife to slice a loaf of bread, and notice how evenly she divides it without seeming to take any special pains to do so. But ask a Capricornian to light a fire and the result is likely to be a dismal failure, no matter how painstakingly they lay the fuel for it. Their role seems to be to damp down rather than inflame the spirits of those around them; you may meet them in a state of euphoria, but before long they are likely to quench your enthusiasm. When angry, they emit icy rather than furious vibrations. Those who attempt to do battle with Capricorn should take warning from this and never give way to hot-headed impulses, for they will be successfully repelled by the Capricornian's coolly calculated self-confidence. The Capricornian does not resort to physical violence, but to other and much more effective ways, to get the better of those who have provoked him beyond endurance.

Forgive and forget is not a Capricornian maxim; he or she will wait long and patiently to work off a grudge.

Like the Cancer-born, Capricorn too lives much in the past – that is why history and archaeology are often favourite subjects with this type. Capricornians have much more faith in whatever has stood the test of time than in what is intended to make for progress. In fact, they hate change and for this reason are apt to get into a rut, becoming hidebound in habits. Only when it is absolutely vital to tear up roots will the Capricornian assent to moving location, cutting completely adrift from familiar surroundings and people. Capricornian success in life is brought about by steadily building up from very solid foundations. Having made a choice of career (and it will be one that is likely to bring gradual self-advancement, rather than offer the prospect of a lightning progress to the top) Capricorn sticks to it. Government posts, and all branches of the Civil Service appeal to this type. If Capricornians go into business it will be of the kind likely to survive any slump in the national economy. You find many of them working on the land, as farmers, breeders of livestock, or horticulturists (they have 'green fingers'); if they enter any of the professions, their choice is likely to be one of the academic ones, law or architecture. There are fewer Sun Capricornians than other types in the fields of art and entertainment, though they are prominent in the musical world (musicians are often very good mathematicians, and Capricornians excel in both capacities).

Capricornians are very careful with money, as has already been hinted, but they will invest freely in property.

Obstinacy, dogmatism, prejudices are temperamental shortcomings of Capricornians. They will not argue about any point at issue between you; instead they maintain a state of silence, which is much more aggravating.

Capricornians are more inclined to be 'loners' than dependent on the companionship of other people. Shy in disposition, reserved in manner, they are very slow to make friends, and most of these are ones shared with other members of the family. Even towards those people with whom they are most intimate they are reticent. It is very difficult for Capricornians to be openly demonstrative of their affection for those near and dear to them, but their devotion is expressed by their protective attitude. As a rule, they are not romantics; they appreciate the people they become attached to because they admire their sterling qualities. Capricornians do not fall in love easily. but when they experience that emotion you can assume that the person they are attracted to is likely to make a reliable, praiseworthy partner. It is said of Capricornians that they are prepared to sacrifice love for ambition and for wealth. I am not so sure that this is true; rather it is the case that the person to whom the Capricornian is attracted just happens to be more successful or more affluent than himself. But though the Capricorn is aware of these advantages, they would count for nothing if he or she is not attuned temperamentally to the individual.

The typical Capricorn is wiry in build, and very bony with especially prominent joints; the head is wide at the top, narrowing towards the chin; the skin is cool and without much colour – it can be pallid; teeth are seldom good (in these days of cosmetic dentistry Capricornians are especially lucrative to the dentist); the nose is prominent, and sometimes curved inwards at the tip; there is something out of proportion about the Capricornian's ears – they are usually larger than average. Capricornians suffer from a poor circulation and a poor digestion; the digestive and eliminative organs function very sluggishly; hands and feet are large.

Though inclined to be somewhat delicate in infancy and early childhood, Capricornians are noted for their longevity. In later life they suffer from rheumatoid ailments; and, if they suffer physical injury, the knees are often involved. They have skin and hair problems.

The Capricorn Man

Very canny; others consider him rather dour, but they rely on his judgment. You find him well up (if not at the top) in any large business corporation – he is very much a 'company man'. Very conservative in his dress, and very old-fashioned in some of his ideas, Capricorn man respects tradition and holds fast to it. You can set your clock by him, he is so regular in his habits. He does not much care for an evening out with the lads; he much prefers to stay home and read a good book, or pass his leisure time there on some course of study. The chances are that he will have a garden he is very proud of, and

ABOVE *The Capricorn man respects tradition, prefers to to stay at home with a good book. He will probably love gardening.*

BELOW *The Capricorn woman is prone to acute depression, is not given to idle gossip but is capable of jealousy.*

which he attends to meticulously. Not lavish with the housekeeping money, he insists that his wife keeps a full account of how she spends it; but she will not go short for anything (barring things he considers to be foolish luxuries), and she can be certain that he will remain faithful to her if she measures up to his standard of what a wife and mother should be. If she fails in either capacity, he will not go out of his way to look for consolation elsewhere, but will become even more absorbed in his career. In any event, she must accept the fact that this takes first place with him.

A disciplinarian where his children are concerned, the Capricorn father is determined to give them a good start in life by providing the best in education for them; but he is not attuned to youth, and this makes communication between him and them very difficult.

Other men may be content to while away their retirement years in idleness; not so Capricorn. If he ends one career around the age of sixty, he is likely to start another. Or you will find him taking a very active role in local politics; he is very politically minded.

The Capricorn Woman

There is nothing flighty about the Capricorn woman; but she can be very attractive to the male species. They admire her brains and her businesslike attitude as well as her good looks. And she can be very good looking – not the chocolate-box type of female, perhaps, but she has very good bone structure and (usually) is very slim, even in later life. In fact, that is often when she looks her best.

She does not have the failings that are attributed to her sex: she is not fickle, or irrational, nor is she the prey of her emotions. But, like her male counterpart, she can be very moody, because she too is prone to bouts of acute depression. She is not the one to indulge in idle

gossip, so her women friends feel safe in confiding in her; nor is she 'catty'. A very economical housekeeper, her home is spotlessly clean but it may not be outstanding for its artistic furnishing. She prefers antiques to modern furniture, quiet, neutral colours to brighter hues. What she buys she buys for its utilitarian value rather than because it appeals to the eye. She hunts around the second-hand shops for bargains, and never makes a mistake about what she selects.

Her partner may feel that she is too unemotional, too pragmatic; but, if he is a sensible fellow, he will stick to her, even though she may not come up to his romantic expectations. Thanks to her, he will do all the better in his career, for she will make it her business to encourage him to make the best of himself. Her children find it difficult to get really close to her, yet they feel all the more secure in their family background because of her; and, though she may suffer in secret when they decide to fly the nest, she will not stand in their way. She knows full well they must learn to make their own way in the world.

Is she capable of jealousy? She is (and so is the Capricorn male); for though they cannot be outwardly

demonstrative, and though they are self-reliant by nature, Capricornians do need to feel secure in their relationship with the few people who mean much to them. But they never make an open display of jealousy – it just makes them even moodier.

The Capricorn Child

A very solemn infant and not, it seems, at all eager to communicate with the world around him. This can be something of a worry to his parents, because he may appear to be backward. It can be certainly very off-putting to adults who drool over his cot; the only response they will get to their efforts is a very cold stare.

At school, the Capricorn boy stands out from the rest of his class because he is so quiet; and the little Capricorn girl is so very tidy. Both have 'old heads on young shoulders' and seem to prefer the company of adults to that of other children. They will make slow but steady progress with their studies, but may show little inclination to join the social side of school life. At most, they will acquire one or two school pals. Even if not happy at school, they will not complain to parents. If you are a Capricorn parent, you will have to take special pains to make sure that your child is not worrying about school and other problems – for Capricornians maintain a poker face and give little or no clue to their feelings.

Not unruly children by any means, they can, however, be very stubborn on occasion; at such times, be patient and try to find out the reason for this. Then, if you discuss the matter calmly with them, they just may be able to see things from your point of view. Do not be too hopeful, though, for Capricornians are the most inflexible of all the zodiac types.

There is no need to teach Capricorn children thrift: they will save most of their pocket money and, given the slightest encouragement, will implement it by making themselves useful to people who are prepared to pay for their services. Also, these children are often skilled in handicrafts. Many show strong scientific leanings. They take great care of their possessions. Given presents, they are likely to store them away for future use. Give them animals as pets, and you will realize just how tender and how patient they can be with them.

You will have no cause to wonder whether you are wasting money on your child's education. Even if Capricorn children do not make spectacular progress before they reach their teens, once they get to college or university their ambition will be to do well. Unlike others who waste their time fooling around, Capricornians will absorb themselves entirely in what they set out to master.

The Capricorn child shows strong scientific leanings and once they get to college or university their ambition will be to do well.

Affinities of Capricorn

Capricorn has an affinity with two of the zodiac types: TAURUS (21 April–20 May), and VIRGO (23 August–22 September). Capricorn gets on well with individuals of these types because they share his practical outlook on life.

Capricorn can establish a close bond of harmony with the 'Water' types (Cancer, Scorpio and Pisces), and often chooses a partner from among them (otherwise the chances are that she will be a Taurean or a Virgoan).

About LIBRA (23 September–22 October) Capricorn has mixed feelings. Can be partly won over by the Libran's charm, but senses that they may be unreliable in emergencies.

Capricorn finds it much harder to get on with some of the other types:

Finds ARIES (21 March–20 April) brash and therefore to be avoided.

GEMINI (21 May–20 June). Capricorn cannot always keep pace with the ideas of these people and dislikes their restless, inquisitive and, in his or her opinion, very immature behaviour.

LEO (23 July–22 August). Capricorn remains immune to the magnetic personality of this type.

SAGITTARIUS (23 November–22 December). Cautious Capricorn is horrified at the risks that Sagittarians take.

AQUARIUS (21 January–19 February). The unpredictability of Aquarians disconcerts Capricorn, who cannot fathom them and just cannot understand why they are so keen to change the old into the new. Nonetheless Capricorn respects Aquarius (and vice-versa) and the two, so different in many ways, can tolerate each other.

AQUARIUS 'THE WATER-BEARER'

Birth period 21 January–19 February

Aquarians are the most complex of all the zodiac types, a bundle of paradoxes and an enigma to the people around them. The symbol of their Sun sign is that of a man (or angel) pouring water from an urn over the earth – but it might just as well be a large question mark. Even the closest relatives of Aquarians will confess that they cannot fathom what is in their mind or what they are likely to say or do next. The general consensus of opinion is that Aquarians are consistent only in their inconsistencies.

Yet, and this is the only one of the many paradoxes of Aquarians, they are not only highly intelligent people but they bring reason to bear on all that they do. Moreover, it is logic backed by the spark of intuition, so that some of the most brilliant thinkers are born under this sign. Aquarius is an 'Air' sign, and as such it has to do with the communication of ideas, and it is the special role of Aquarians to spread knowledge to the greater benefit of mankind – not only material benefit, but the spiritual kind too, enabling man to evolve to his highest state of being.

Humanitarianism is the principle of Aquarius, and Aquarians are humanitarians at heart. For them, there are no distinctions of race, colour or creed – and the typical Aquarian firmly believes that all mankind should enjoy equal rights. This is why you find the Aquarian linked with organizations, groups and movements that work for the common good. Indeed, in the individual horoscopes of the founders of such movements Aquarius and its part-ruler, Uranus, are usually prominent. Those Aquarians who are gifted in the arts make them a medium for propagating their humane ideas. One example was Charles Dickens who did more, through his novels, to stir the conscience of the Victorians on behalf of the poor than most of the other notable do-gooders of his generation.

But, although the average Aquarian is so well-disposed to people *en masse*, has hosts of acquaintances and many friends, he fights shy of completely identifying himself with the people with whom he becomes involved. For, above all, Aquarians are the prime individualists of the zodiac, who feel compelled to guard their own identity, their own personal freedom at all costs; and it is this that creates an invisible yet impregnable barrier between them and the people who try to get very close to them.

That barrier is created by the Aquarian's dispassionate nature: kindhearted but not warmhearted. It is impossible for the Aquarian (unless there are other very powerful factors at work in his or her horoscope) to experience the ardent feelings, the romantic ecstasy, or the emotional dependence on other people that is characteristic of the 'Water' zodiac types, or even the powerful feelings common to the people born under the 'Fire' sign. The closest bond between the typical Aquarian and any individual will be one based on an intellectual affinity. Aquarius loves with the mind rather than with the heart.

In some respects, this can be a blessing for the Aquarian's partner and children. For it prevents the Aquarians from becoming possessive towards anyone of whom they are fond; there will be no outbursts of jealousy, no attempt to monopolize the affections of those nearest and dearest to them. In fact, spouse and children may be left in doubt about how much the Aquarian cares for them, for though forthcoming on other matters, Aquarians are not given to expressing their feelings of affection. In this, they very much resemble inarticulate Capricorn.

There are exceptions, of course, and Charles Dickens was one. He was (like so many Victorians) mawkishly sentimental on occasion – and he had an unfortunate habit of falling in love much too easily and too often. But that was because he had Venus in the very romantic sign of Pisces.

For most Aquarians, though, platonic relationships with the opposite sex are infinitely preferable to the other kind. The Aquarian male pays women the compliment of appreciating them for their intelligence rather than their looks. That is not to say he does not enjoy the company of those who are easy on the eye, but they will not prise him away from the woman who is witty, brainy, and who can converse with him at his own level on his pet topics – she beats any competitors, even if she has a deplorable figure and a face like an old boot.

Though not passionate by disposition, Aquarians are certainly loyal to their friends and associates, and they make this very clear to any potential mischief-makers. Aquarius is no fair-weather friend who fades away when you are in trouble; and Aquarians though they may not even like you, if they feel you are being unfairly attacked they will certainly speak up for you. This stems from the Aquarian's impartial attitude to other people. 'Treat them all alike' is the Aquarian's motto, and this applies to both working relationships and personal relationships.

The Aquarian is very single-minded about whatever he or she becomes interested in or aims to do. But the Aquarian driving force functions spasmodically – they will produce tremendous bouts of effort, but these will be interspersed with lethargic phases. There is another odd thing about Aquarians. Having striven hard and in the face of recurrent setbacks to reach any goal they have in view, once it is attained they often lose all interest in it. Many Aquarians have thrown up a career just when they have reached the peak of success in order to go off at a tangent on a course that is full of hazards. But you can be sure it will be something that allows them to test their capabilities to a much greater extent.

The Aquarian is, it seems, in a perpetual state of growing – self-development never reaches a final stage with this type. So, if you want to maintain the Aquarian's interest, you too will have to present him or her with new facets of your personality, fresh evidence of your skills. Aquarians have no time for people who get into a rut – which, to the Aquarian, is the worst possible fate that could befall anyone.

Careers that present many challenges appeal to Aquarians, those that give scope for creative thought, technological expertise, and those that demand very highly specialized qualifications. Science has a very special appeal, for the Aquarian is a scientific observer of nature – including human nature; but you will also find the Aquarian in all branches of the arts. Aquarians are not really business-minded, yet many gravitate into industry. But they do so in areas that do not demand financial acumen but rather the technical know-how to improve the product, or the right ideas for improving the service offered.

When it comes to handling money Aquarians go from one extreme to the other. They skimp on essentials but will part with what seem to others exorbitant sums for what takes their fancy. And it is the Aquarians who leave their wealth to some kind of charitable institution (very probably one to do with animals, for Aquarians are animal lovers and very active in the prevention of cruelty to animals). Relatives, on the other hand, stand a poor chance of mention in the Aquarian's will. The sad thing is that so many Aquarians drift away completely from their relatives even if they do not quarrel with them. Aquarians do not quarrel: they just cut you out of their lives completely if you have done anything to offend them deeply, without even giving you the satisfaction of knowing why they have done so.

Aquarians have sound physical constitutions – this is one of the zodiac types with above-average life expectation. Aquarians may seem very urbane in manner – and they never 'flap' when faced with a crisis – but, for all that, they have a very highly sensitive nervous system. However, their dispassionate nature prevents them from suffering the acute nervous disorders common to other types. What they do suffer from is a 'spasmodic' circulation – this may confuse the doctor, for it imposes strain on the heart at times and the stethoscope will then record heart flutters. Organically, the Aquarian's heart is as sound as a bell. Hardening of the arteries, varicose veins, swollen ankles – all the symptoms of circulatory problems do tend to show themselves as the Aquarian gets older. But Aquarians are blessed in that their mental faculties remain unimpaired.

Aquarians are delightful in youth, and they are still fascinating in middle age; but they can become very cranky and eccentric in later life. Actually, those eccentricities were there all the time, but they seemed merely amusing, or a source of extra fascination to others while the Aquarian was young or still in the prime of life. The Aquarian gets a lot of secret amusement out of disconcerting other people (especially those who are very conservative, very conventional) by saying or doing things that will outrage them. There is a very impish streak, indeed a childish streak in Aquarians.

By now the reader perhaps has a fuller picture of the average Aquarian, but it is by no means a complete one. No astrologer could adequately describe all the quirks that go to make up the Aquarian character and personality. As for the Aquarian life history, almost invariably it develops along very unusual lines and comprises a series of totally disconnected episodes. As Aquarians are keen on travel, it usually forms an important feature of their life history; and most prefer the country to town life. They may put down what seem to be deep roots,

but these will be torn up every so often.

Marriage is a gamble; for though Aquarians are not prone to infidelity, their temperament is such that marital life is a very severe test for them. It will have all the more chance of becoming an enduring relationship if the Aquarian is able to spend periods away from home every so often, either travelling for career purposes, or spending some time in solitude in a quiet retreat. When it was very much against the rules of society to settle down with someone without seeking the blessing of the Church first, Aquarians would openly defy convention – and their irregular unions fared well. Now that we are in a permissive age, we find that they are very adamant indeed about sealing the partnership, if not in Church, then in the registry office: this, nowadays, is the unconventional thing.

Physically, Aquarians are among the good-lookers of the zodiac: well-built, with very classical features and a good bone structure, even if it is a little on the large side. The Aquarian eyes are a specially arresting feature as they glow with an inner radiance; almost almond-shaped, they tilt at the corners. At times, the Aquarians have a very dreamy look, at others they seem to be very amused by what they see; they never have a disagreeable look, even when they are put out about something. The skin is translucent, the hair is usually fine, and maybe very curly. Aquarian hands are elegant, with beautiful, filbert-shaped nails and long, slim eloquent fingers. The odd thing about the Aquarian's mode of conversation is that it seems to be interspersed with *non sequiturs* – the Aquarian mind has suddenly veered off at a tangent.

Aquarians are not domesticated by nature and, if left to do their own housekeeping, will reduce it to a minimum. But one feature their home will have: plenty of electrical gadgets. Uranus is the planet to do with electricity, and many Aquarians (and not merely the men) are intensely interested in electronics and often choose this as a career. They are also gifted inventors – but too often they are careless about patenting what they invent, and thus fail to reap the financial rewards.

Aquarians can be very faddy about food – this is indeed the only thing they may have in common with Virgo, with whom they will discuss natural foods and diets *ad infinitum*.

The Aquarian Man

The more affluent Aquarian man is very much a clubman, and likely to spend much more time at his clubs than at home; if a bachelor, he may prefer to make one his *pied-à-terre* rather than set up house elsewhere. If, however, he does decide to do so, he is apt to choose the most unlikely (and, in the opinion of other people, most unsuitable) quarters. He has some very odd ideas of furnishing a home – many of the items he acquires will probably be used for any purpose rather than the one they were intended for.

Unless he follows a totally independent course in his career, he likes to associate himself with some kind of large organization, in either case, a born organizer. Being very progressive in his ideas and methods, he has no difficulty in outstripping business or professional competitors. Not that he deliberately sets out to do so – it is natural for him to keep a step ahead.

Aquarian man is someone who is in a perpetual state of

with him, as he shows no desire to form strong attachments and treats all friends with complete impartiality. Women are fascinated by him, and he enjoys their company. But, unless there are other reasons for this in his individual horoscope, he is not a passionate lover – and his girlfriend or wife will find it a very frustrating experience if she tries to make him jealous by flirting with other men.

He will discuss anything and everything under the sun with you, but if the discussion becomes an argument and he is getting the worst of it he will skilfully sidetrack you with another topic.

Even if the nature of his work forces him to submit to routine, the Aquarius man will manage to vary it – his personal life is never a matter of routine. Do not expect him willingly to make arrangements far in advance – he prefers to act on impulse. Do not expect him to be punctual when it comes to keeping appointments; he will either turn up too early, or when you have given up any hope of seeing him. If he says he is going out to get a packet of cigarettes you may have to wait in vain for his return. Yet, when you finally think he has gone out of your life for ever, likely as not he will turn up again.

His life history would make good material for a fascinating biography: it is one of disconnected episodes, and very, very out of the ordinary.

The Aquarian Woman

She is very much a committee woman, and takes an active part when it comes to anything that is organized for the benefit of the community – she will probably be running the show. But you would not give her top marks for running a home – she spends too much time elsewhere.

The Aquarian woman lacks many of the wiles, and foibles, that supposedly characterize her sex: she is not inclined to be jealous of other women; she does not resort to the little tricks that other women use to captivate the male – and she is certainly not a clinging vine. Men respect her for her ability to think the way they do, and because she is so self-reliant. They realize, however, that they cannot take her for granted, and this keeps her boyfriend or husband all the more under her spell. She is at her best when dealing with an emergency; very courageous when the occasion demands a brave front.

She is also a careerist by temperament (like the Aries female); and she is certainly politically minded. Very many women scientists are born with this sign prominent in their horoscopes. She is keen to bring up her children on 'modern' lines; unlike so many other mothers, she does not delude herself that they are superior to other children, but she will certainly do her best to stimulate their intelligence. She gives them plenty of scope to express their own individuality, but becomes irritated if they show signs of becoming too independent of her. However, she is not the sort to protest when her children express a desire to fly the nest; and she can be counted upon to be gracious to whoever they fall in love with. As a mother-in-law, she earns the gratitude of whoever her children marry because she makes no attempt to intrude into their territory.

The Aquarian woman is always ready to make her partner's friends and acquaintances welcome when he brings them home without warning, and she is not at all discomforted if visitors turn up when her home is not

The Aquarian man, a born organizer, will discuss anything and everything under the sun and is very, very out of the ordinary.

self-development, mentally and spiritually. He is very much an idealist, and not very materialistic – this is why he may not fully capitalize on his talents. He prefers to leave the purely financial side of business to others. Ask him to subscribe to a good cause and he is likely to do so generously; ask him to lend you five pounds and you will probably get a curt refusal; he adheres strongly to the advice 'never a borrower or a lender be'. He might, however, *give* you the fiver.

Although other men admire him for his intellect and his wit, they find it impossible to get on very close terms looking its best, for she is quite indifferent to what their impressions of it may be.

There is always something very distinctive about the way she dresses. No slave to fashion, she wears what appeals to her regardless of whether it suits her. Usually, though, she has good taste – up to a point; but what would otherwise be a perfect ensemble will as likely as not be spoiled by an incongruous detail.

One of her most refreshing qualities is that there is nothing petty about her. She can, like the Aquarian man, be very contrary, but she is not mean-spirited.

The Aquarian woman is often a scientist, gives her children plenty of scope to develop their own individuality and will not protest when they express a desire to leave the nest. She is not upset if visitors turn up unexpectedly at her home.

Other women are sometimes perplexed by the cool manner in which she can accept infidelity on the part of her partner; but, for her, it is much more important to be able to regard him as a friend than as a lover. He, of course, feels that he will never get to know her completely: that would be impossible for anyone who becomes involved with an Aquarian.

The Aquarian Child

Because Aquarians are basically amiable in disposition, even if independent, the self-willed side of their nature will not be especially stressed during infancy and early childhood. In fact, Aquarians are particularly good-tempered babies – you will hear them crooning contentedly to themselves while they play with the toys you have provided.

Once they begin to crawl they become very explorative, so you will have to keep an eye open for their whereabouts. It is no use putting them into a playpen: the Aquarian child hates to be fenced in; much better to obtain one of those old-fashioned 'strollers' that enables them to move freely and you to keep them within sight. If put among other children, they will be friendly enough, but very quick to move away if their playmates try to take hold of them. The chances are that your Aquarian child will learn to read at a very early age and become keenly interested in books.

The more progressive type of school is preferable for Aquarians, and it should if possible be co-educational: this may help to make your youngster take a closer interest in the opposite sex, which they are otherwise unlikely to do until they reach their late teens or even early twenties. For the sex drive, never very emphasized in this type, is usually completely dormant until early adult life, and this makes it all the more awkward for them to bridge the gap between adolescence and adulthood.

There is no need to fear that your child will be unhappy if you send him or her to boarding school, provided it is one in which discipline is not too pronounced. The Aquarian is not very closely attached to the family, so there will be no pangs of homesickness. The Aquarian child will participate in the sports and social side of school life, but in a mildly interested way. He or she will be much more interested in spending time in the school laboratory or craft centre. Amateur theatricals will, however, hold a special appeal – the Aquarian will like to organize and direct them, and maybe write the plays for them.

Young Aquarians are keen on hobbies, but not the kind that usually claim children's interest. You will not be bothered with pleas for extra pocket money: little Aquarians are no spendthrifts, though they may develop some expensive tastes later.

Tidiness is not usually one of the virtues of Aquarians; visitors are best steered quickly past your child's door.

72

Punctuality is not an Aquarian virtue either, so that is another problem that has to be sorted out. How to do so? Not by criticizing, but by making excuses for both faults – if you emphasize that you quite understand that your young Aquarian cannot overcome these failings, he or she will, contrarily, decide to prove how wrong you are.

Affinities of Aquarius

Aquarius reacts favourably to the following zodiac types:

ARIES (21 March–20 April). Aquarians have no difficulty at all in maintaining friendly relations with Arians, even though the latter are so hotheaded and argumentative. Aquarius is amused by Aries' recklessness and skilfully sidesteps the provocative Arian tactics.

LEO (23 July–22 August). There is often a very strong bond between Leo and Aquarius, as might be expected where there is the attraction of opposites: the contrast here is between the Aquarian's preference for being the power behind the scenes, and the Leo's love of openly exercising authority – encouraged by Aquarius, so long as it serves the latter's humanitarian aims. This brings to mind another curious trait of Aquarians. They believe everyone should have the right to think and act for himself, yet they like to influence the thoughts and actions of others – with the best of intentions – and Leo is the perfect instrument.

LIBRA (23 September–22 October). Aquarius finds Librans very refreshing company, so long as they do not become too dependent. But when Librans resort to their characteristically artful attempts to manipulate Aquarius they never succeed: the latter just fades gently out.

SAGITTARIUS (23 November–22 December). This type is especially liked by Aquarius. Sagittarians never make demands on Aquarians, and both have wide-ranging minds so that they find delight in discussing their many mutual topics of interest.

CAPRICORN (23 December–20 January). With this type a lasting association can be established. Capricornians admire the intellectual gifts of the Aquarians and their dispassionate attitude; Aquarians respect the strength of character and stoicism of Capricorn, even though the latter's old-fashioned ideas and dislike of change are not in accord with the Aquarian outlook. This is a good instance of the Aquarian policy of maintaining a friendly if detached attitude when points of affinity are able to compensate for differences on other matters.

PISCES (20 February–20 March). Aquarius is unfailingly kind to Pisces, who is eternally fascinated by the former's unpredictability, while quite unable to understand how anyone could be so lacking in warmth of feeling. However, it is a great comfort for Pisces, landed in yet another predicament, to be able to turn for advice to Aquarius, whose original manner of viewing situations will point the way out when no one else can.

Aquarius has little or no affinity with these four types:

TAURUS (21 April–20 May) and VIRGO (23 August–22 September). These two types have little in common with Aquarius, who is exasperated by the Taurean's pre-occupation with purely material values and limited range of ideas and interests, and also by the Virgoan's proneness to worry: Aquarius is an optimist who never worries. Virgo also makes the mistake of pointing out and criticizing Aquarian inconsistencies. This is resented, for Aquarians are in fact unconscious of being in the wrong: whatever they say or do seems right to them at the time.

GEMINI (21 May–20 June). Though they share the same sense of fun, Geminians irritate Aquarius because they cannot stick to the truth. Aquarians cannot bear being told even harmless untruths and they become mistrustful of Gemini's glib tongue.

SCORPIO (23 October–22 November). A type that Aquarius tends to avoid. Scorpio's passionate nature, intense jealousy and blunt ways are anathema to the Aquarian.

The Aquarian child participates in sports and amateur theatricals hold a special appeal.

PISCES 'THE FISHES'

Birth period 20 February–20 March

It is just as well that nobody can possess all the characteristics of his Sun sign, otherwise one wonders just what would happen to Pisceans. As it is, they seem to find it impossible to run their lives on simple, well-organized lines. They get into extraordinary predicaments for which they have nobody to blame but themselves, and it is usually their good intentions rather than dubious motives that land them in trouble.

Kindly, compassionate, capable of much self-sacrifice, not merely for the sake of duty but because they are filled with love towards all mankind, Pisceans are also self-indulgent to the extent that in order to gratify the impulse of the moment they will totally ignore their obligations. They will suffer agonies of remorse for their lapses from grace, yet seem unable to exercise the will power to overcome their weaknesses, without the strong moral support of people who exercise a good influence on them.

More than any other of the zodiac types, Pisceans are dependent on help from others to bring out the best in themselves. But they are so impressionable, so submissive in attitude to others that they all too easily come under the sway of the people who encourage them to stray from the path of virtue. In fact Pisceans seem to be particularly attracted to those who will lead them down the road to ruin. This is because it is impossible for Pisceans to think badly of anyone, conscious as they are of their own failings.

The strongest motivating urge in the average Piscean is to live life and enjoy it to the full. The smallest pleasures of life give them infinite satisfaction: they get as much enjoyment out of a bus ride around the town or through the countryside as they would out of a world tour. They may like champagne, but a glass of shandy will equally please their palate. They manage to get as much fun out of life when they do not have two ha'pennies to rub together as they do when there is plenty of money for luxuries and amusements. However, Pisceans are seldom hard up for long: they tend to be lucky in money matters – and anyway there is always someone on hand to tide them over their lean times. The nicest thing about them is that they will share everything they have with you, or even give you all they possess to make you happy.

There is such a fluid quality to the Piscean nature that people get very confused impressions about the type. In fact, unconsciously Pisceans take on the attitudes, habits and mannerisms of whoever they become closely attached to. The symbol of the sign is that of two fishes trying to swim their opposite ways but unable to do so because they are joined together. Actually, the Piscean nature is not only a dual one, but changeable. That is why the Pisces man can be all things to all men.

It is said of the more highly evolved Pisceans that they are in tune with the Infinite, and most have strong spiritual yearnings; it is as though they have a foot in two worlds, for they are intuitively conscious of supernatural forces for which there is no rational explanation.

Pisces is the sign of mysticism and, in terms of organized religions, it is the sign of Christianity (the early Christians made themselves known to each other during the time of their persecution by outlining the symbol of the fishes).

On the other hand, the Piscean is as much a bon viveur as a mystic. I know one who alternates regularly between nightclubs and discotheques and places of retreat provided by religious orders for peaceful seclusion and spiritual reflection.

One of the vices that the Piscean does avoid like the plague is the desire to exercise power. Pisceans have no desire whatever to dictate to others; and though they will yield willingly to gentle persuasion, they will manage to escape from the clutches of anyone who becomes too domineering.

How do they manage to do so? Even the slipperiest of fishes fails to squirm out of the net or shake free of the bait he has swallowed. Pisceans perform the miracle by managing to do in secret what they are not permitted to do openly. For, being by nature timid, Pisceans express their rebellious reactions only by resorting to subtle, secretive tactics. This secretive streak is one they share with the other two 'Water' types of the zodiac. So do not imagine that you will ever be able to boast that you have plumbed the depths of the Piscean's nature – there is always something of himself, his desires and hopes that will remain unkown to you.

Intuition, imagination, and versatility are Piscean qualities; and all find constructive outlets in their interests and activities. Ideally, the occupations for people born under this sign are those where they have full scope for analytical and deductive powers, for artistic inclinations. You will find them in all branches of the arts; in particular they excel as actors. They not only take on a role, they live it, and they can assume any role, even though they have an aversion to the more unpleasant ones – it goes against the grain for them to portray villains, but they will put up a wonderful performance all the same.

Pisceans do equally well in the professions and in the world of commerce and industry; for though careless and extravagant in handling their own finances, many have considerable business acumen. But, though Pisceans rise to high positions in these spheres, you seldom find them heading the board of a company – Pisces never wants the responsibility of ultimate authority, and can also be extremely modest about putting talents on display.

There is, however, one particular type of profession that not only enables Pisceans to use their intelligence and acquired skills to best purpose, but provides the means for greatest self-fulfilment. As doctors, nurses, welfare workers – and, if they follow their strong religious inclinations, as missionaries – they become the most dedicated workers for the common good of humanity. More than anything else, a humane vocation will help Pisceans to develop the strength of character they otherwise lack.

Having an affinity with water, it is only natural that the Piscean may choose to earn a livelihood by turning to marine or aquatic occupations. But the self-indulgent, easy-going Piscean may also resort to gambling. The world of advertising, which thrives on encouraging the public at large to buy what it neither needs nor can afford, needs the services of people skilled in glamourizing products – and Pisceans are particularly good at devising advertising campaigns with great pulling power.

The personal lives of Pisceans would provide rich material for the romantic novelist – falling in and out of love is one of the regular pastimes of people born under this sign. Pisceans never outgrow the idealistic attitude to romance that they cherish in their youth; and, no matter how many times romance fails to come up to expectations, they remain hopeful that the latest love affair will be the one that will bring the ultimate in happiness. So indiscriminate are they in bestowing their affections that it is not uncommon for Pisceans to have several romances in hand at a time. Pisceans do not much care about taking on marital responsibilities, though once they have done so they will strive to carry them out. As a rule, though, it is the Piscean's partner who takes over the lion's share of responsibilities, if only for the sake of enjoying some degree of material security. Pisces can be easily persuaded to let him or her control the budget, make the decisions, and do all the organizing necessary to keep the domestic establishment running on smooth lines.

Though very vulnerable to passing infatuations, Pisces is capable of being completely loyal to his or her mate so long as there is a bond of love between them. If love flies out of the window, the Piscean's fidelity will follow suit very quickly. But infidelities are practised very discreetly, mainly because kindhearted Pisceans do not like to hurt the feelings of their partner.

Even in these days of careful family planning, Pisceans prefer to have large families. The more people they have around them to love and be loved by, the happier they are. As parents, they make no attempt to discipline their children, but the youngsters are usually very well behaved, for to be able to give love so abundantly is to receive it in full measure in return, and this is expressed in the good behaviour of the children of Pisces.

Pisceans are not very robust people; they are particularly vulnerable to infectious ailments, and for this reason have to guard their own health when in contact with people suffering from such illnesses. That is the one handicap for the Pisceans who wish to take up nursing – they must stick to dealing with patients with non-contagious ailments. They love good food and, it must be admitted, are very fond of alcohol. Pisceans' health problems are dietary ones. They put on weight all too easily, and their liver reacts very quickly to abuse. Not especially fond of exercise, Pisceans need to take more of it to keep in good shape. They are also more inclined to have a glandular imbalance than most of the other types. People born under this sign usually have a special addiction to shellfish, but should be particularly careful to guard against food poisoning – in fact, of all the zodiac types, Pisceans are most subject to blood disorders brought on by eating what does not agree with them.

Physical appearance of course depends upon various factors in an individual horoscope (to say nothing of the hereditary factor); but the typical Piscean is of average height, or below it, with limbs that are disproportionately short to the body. A full, wide forehead, arched brows, very large soulful eyes (they can resemble a bloodhound's when the Piscean is in a melancholy mood), rounded cheeks, a sensitive mouth and a soft, pale skin are the distinctive physical characteristics of this type. Though often very graceful dancers, their normal walking gait is less impressive – it sometimes resembles that of a penguin. There is something fishlike too in the outline of the Piscean. The part of the body ruled by Pisces are the feet, and they can be troublesome to Pisceans – breaking in new shoes is agony for them, so do not imagine they have sunk to the poverty line if their shoes are falling apart.

Pisceans love to travel, especially by sea; given the opportunity, they will make their home on a houseboat, or choose a house close to water. Pisceans love swimming and diving, and will tolerate the claustrophobic atmosphere of a submarine without any show of fear, but paradoxically they are especially prone to catching colds if they live or work in low-lying districts and, if exposed to them too long, may suffer from more serious respiratory trouble, such as chronic bronchitis.

They should be particularly cautious about taking any form of medical drug, for they of all types become most quickly addicted. Similarly, the use of anaesthetics is to be avoided, if possible, by the doctor dealing with a Pisces patient: they 'go under' easily enough, but take so long to return to consciousness that it may cause a great deal of anxiety.

The Pisces Man

He is very popular with other men: they may think him a rather weak character, but they are impressed by his knowledge of food and wine; they know he can be trusted to keep a secret if they confide in him; he is always ready to help out with a loan of cash, always ready to go off on a spree – and what good company he can be for a night out on the tiles. He has a bawdy sense of humour, but never makes a display of it in mixed company. He is popular with his parish priest, too; for he will always support charities with money and with active participation. And unlike other men, he is prepared to discuss theological matters at some length, and is surprisingly knowledgeable. The vicar knows him well enough, however, not to take him too seriously when he seems inclined to give up the rat race in favour of retiring to a monastery.

The Pisces man is shrewd when it comes to advising his business friends about stocks and shares, yet they find, to their surprise, that he has not seized the same opportunity himself. The fact is, he is probably short of money at the time, and his bank manager is taking a firm line about his overdraft. However, he does make money – and in a very big way – from various sources, but he never holds on to it for long.

He is very gallant in plying the particular lady he is taking out with little tokens of his appreciation: he never fails to provide her with a first-class meal, the best type of transport, a gift of flowers or chocolates (or both). The chances are that she will be forced to refuse, for the sake of form, much costlier gifts. Unlike some of the other zodiac males, he will take it very good-humouredly if she accepts his offerings without giving him more than companionship in return.

The Piscean male is kind to old people, and particularly so to the handicapped and under-privileged. He does the gentlemanly thing, too, and treats his wife and his mistress with the same courtesy and consideration – taking good care that the latter is kept in ignorance of the existence of the former.

He is not always able to resist the temptation to involve himself in deals that are far from above-board – it is this that lands him in hot water.

The Pisces Woman

She is very much the type of woman men love to be with, not only because of her sex appeal (and she oozes it) but because she is such a good listener, so sympathetic when they feel in need of comfort, so tolerant of their shortcomings, so ready to forgive and forget if they do her wrong. Other women envy her popularity with men and wonder why she turns down so many opportunities to make a really good marriage in favour of a mate who will clearly be a burden rather than a source of strength. She feels she can change him, turn his failures to successes, change his bad traits into good ones. What is more, he is so much more attractive than those staid fellows who

The Pisces man has an appreciation of good food and wine, he does make money but never holds on to it for long because he is too fond of spending it on gifts for the 'particular lady'.

Even if he keeps his nose clean in all business or professional relationships, he may have his reputation undermined through no fault of his own by allowing himself to be seen to associate with people who have no reputation to lose. Rogues can have charming personalities and Pisces succumbs to their charms, shutting his eyes to their disreputable activities.

The Piscean male will probably have a chequered life, but it will certainly be a very colourful one. It rises to the peak of success and plummets to disaster by turns because Pisces is apt to lean too heavily on his Jupiterian luck, and ignore the danger signals of Neptune – Jupiter and Neptune being the co-rulers of his Sun sign.

have been courting her. Piscean women do have a habit of preferring the male sinners to the saints.

The Pisces woman is not a methodical housewife: in fact, if forced to run the home unaided, her husband must be prepared to put up with eternal disorder there. But there is a very happy, relaxing atmosphere at home; he is free of any nagging there – even if he has to spend too much of his precious free time sorting out the mess she has made of the household accounts: she has lost all those bills he needs to present to his accountant, she is unable to keep within her housekeeping allowance, but a few tears at the right moment will melt her husband's heart and he parts with yet more cash than he can

*The Pisces woman is not thrifty and often buys toys for her children,
but a few tears will melt her husband's heart.*

afford. Likely as not, even though she intended it for her own use, she will spend it on special treats for the children (she spoils them to a ridiculous extent). Her moods change so rapidly that others cannot keep pace with them, but this makes her all the more appealing to her partner.

The Pisces Child

A gentle, loving child, very sensitive, very imaginative, a dreamer, young Pisces needs lots of encouragment to face up to life. Very prone to tears: this is the little Piscean's method of defence; for when he or she looks at you with those tear-filled eyes you are in no mood to be severe, even if your youngster has been particularly mischievous. These children mature much later than most of the other zodiac types – do not try to wean them away from their childish ways too soon. On the other hand, you must encourage your Piscean offspring to be more reliant, to think and act for themselves; and most of all you must insist that they cultivate tidy habits.

Other children tend to be protective towards them – any child who tries to bully Pisces will soon be dealt with by other youngsters; Pisceans bring out a protective quality in other people right from the cradle.

Pisceans find it difficult to distinguish between reality and fantasy. Your child will be living in the world of his or her imagination for most of the time – and a delightful world it is. However, you will have to see to it that your Piscean child does not resort to untruths when he has done something he knows you will disapprove of; this type of child must be taught how important it is to be truthful if he is to retain the faith of other people.

School reports may leave much to be desired – they will not be reports of bad behaviour, but almost certainly the comment at the end of them will be 'does not try hard enough' or 'gives up too easily'. However, if you attend any entertainment given by the school for the parents you will certainly feel proud of your Piscean son or daughter, who will shine in any such display of talent.

At the adolescent stage, your Piscean child will have harmless 'crushes'. Do not laugh at them – Pisces just cannot help falling in love, even if it is only calf love.

As this is a sign of the zodiac especially linked with the arts and entertainments, it might be as well, if your Piscean child shows any special artistic talent, to send him or her to a school where the normal type of education is combined with specialized artistic training. Do not send Piscean children to a school where the discipline is lax. Schools with a denominational background are particularly suitable for Pisceans, for their emphasis on religious teaching will help them to overcome the weaknesses in their character.

Piscean children love pets, and giving them pets will help them to shoulder responsibilities conscientiously; it is also the best way of teaching them the facts of life (otherwise, in view of their own vivid imagination, and the garbled versions that other youngsters may give them, they are likely to get some very odd ideas about sex).

It is very important indeed that these children feel really secure in their family background – remember how intuitive they are. They will quickly sense if there is any disharmony between the parents. Do not, unless absolutely forced to, send them to boarding school – you need to keep a careful eye on the company that young Pisceans keep, and you will not be able to do this if they live away from home. This child comes much too easily under the influence of youngsters who could lead them into bad habits and trouble.

Affinities of Pisces

One of the 'Fire' types, SAGITTARIUS (23 November–22 December), is a good associate for Pisces. Although at times the very high-spirited, adventurous impulses of this type may encourage Pisceans to recklessness, Sagittarians help Pisceans out of those moods of deep depression and the sense of inadequacy that overtake them from time to time. Pisceans seem unable to maintain a good emotional balance, alternating between bouts of euphoria and the profoundest gloom.

The two 'Earth' types TAURUS (21 April–20 May) and CAPRICORN (23 December–20 January) also have a specially good effect on Pisces. The practical, down-to-earth attitude of both types brings the Piscean, who spends far too much time in the realms of dream and fantasy, back to the realities of life.

CANCER (21 June–22 July) and SCORPIO (23 October–22 November) adopt a protective attitude to Pisces. As friends and partners they know just how to handle the Piscean.

Pisces have difficulty in getting on with the following:

GEMINI (21 May–20 June) and LIBRA (23 September–22 October) enjoy the company of Pisceans, but neither do much to help them overcome their failings. Gemini is much too restless and lacks the emotional sensitivity to respond to the Piscean need to give full play to sentimental impulses, often making the mistake of treating these in an offhand way. Librans are themselves too easy-going: they and Pisceans encourage each other into greater self-indulgence.

VIRGO (23 August–22 September). Although they do their best to help Pisceans, Virgoans all too often make life more of a trial for them. Virgo is more inclined to criticize than encourage Pisces with praise for making efforts to live up to Virgoan standards of behaviour. Pisces becomes disheartened by constant nagging and gives up altogether, so both types end up completely frustrated.

AQUARIUS (21 January–19 February) is as detached towards Pisces as to other zodiac types. However, Aquarians realize that Pisceans are full of good intentions. They therefore do their best to reinforce the Pisceans' confidence in their ability to fulfil these good intentions. But, though fascinated by the Aquarian's striking individuality, Pisceans feel that Aquarians are lacking in sentiment.

ARIES (21 March–20 April), is dealt with last here because Pisceans have mixed feelings towards this type. They admire the courage of Arians, but are apt to feel nervous of their fiery characteristics. If Aries flies into a rage, Pisces retreats. This aggravates Aries, who likes nothing better than a good fight, whereas Pisces is essentially a pacifist and will not retaliate. In time Aries comes to despise Pisces; well aware of this, the latter shies away all the more, feeling completely demoralized by the Ram's scorn.

The Pisces child often has a special artistic talent and is a great lover of pets.

79

INDEX

Air signs; Gemini, 27–30;
 Libra, 47–51; Aquarius,
 69–73
Aquarian Age, 14
Aquarius 'The Water-
 Bearer': sign of
 humanitarianism and
 brotherhood, 14; signs, 15;
 personality, 69–70;
 Water-Bearer Symbol of,
 69; Air sign, 69, Man,
 70–71; Woman, 71–2;
 Child, 72–3; Affinities, 73
Aratus of Soli, composed
 detailed descriptions of
 known constellations in
 verse, 10
Aries 'The Ram'; signs, 14;
 personality, 17; Fire sign,
 17; Ram symbol of, 17;
 Man, 17, 19; Woman, 19;
 Child, 19; Affinities, 20
Aristotelian theory;
 immaterial to astrology, 12
Astrology: in early religions,
 7; in development of
 civilization, 7; basis of, 7;
 history of, 7–14; beginnings
 in Mesopotamia, 7; in
 Babylon, 7; in Egypt, 8–9;
 in Greece, 9–10; in Rome,
 10; in medieval and
 renaissance times, 10–12;
 challenged by Christianity,
 10; in post renaissance
 times, 12; in East and
 New World, 13; in modern
 times, 13–14
Astronomy, 7; advances in,
 12
Augustus, Emperor, 10

Babylon: astrology in, 7–8;
 temple-observatories in,
 8; boundary stones in, 8
Berosus, Babylonian priest, 8
Biological rhythms: 13

Cancer 'The Crab': on
 Babylonian stone, 8; signs,
 14; personality, 31–33;
Crab symbol of, 31; Water
 sign, 33; Man, 33;
 Woman, 33–4; Child,
 35–6; Affinities, 36
Capricorn 'The Goat': on
 Babylonian boundary
 stone, 8; on Roman coin
 of Augustus, 10; signs, 14;

personality, 63, 65; Goat
 symbol of, 63; Earth sign,
 63; Man, 65–6; Woman,
 66; Child, 67; Affinities, 67
Celestial Atlases, 12
Chicory: a flower associated
 with Sagittarius, 56
China, astrology in, 13
Copernicus, 12
Crawford, Joan: typical
 Arian, 19

Dandelion: a flower
 associated with Libra, 15
Davies, Bette: typical Arian,
 19
Dickens, Charles: typical
 Aquarian, 69

Earth signs: Taurus, 21–5;
 Virgo, 43–6; Capricorn,
 63–7
Egypt: astrology in, 8–9;
 horoscopes in, 9; solar
 calendar in, 9; twelve
 signs of Zodiac regularized
 in, 9
Elements (Fire, Earth, Air,
 Water), 9
Ephemerides, 14

Fire signs: Aries, 17–20;
 Leo, 37–41; Sagittarius,
 57–62
Forces: natural, 6; animate
 and inanimate, 6

Gemini 'The Twins': signs,
 14; personality, 27–8;
 Twins symbol of, 27; Air
 sign, 27; Man, 28–9;
 Woman, 29–30; Affinities,
 30
Greece: philosophers in, 9;
 Astrology in, 9–10

Halley's Comet, *13*
Horoscopes: 7; in Babylon,
 8; astrologers, 8; in Egypt,
 9; in Greece, 10;
 calculation of individual,
 14; analysis of, 15
Houses: 9, 14, 15

India, astrology in, 13

John of Holywood, author
 of first astrological
 textbook in Western

Europe, 12
Jupiter, 15; planetary ruler
 of Sagittarius, 57; part-
 ruler of Pisces, 77

Kidinnus, Babylonian priest
 (*c*. 400 BC), 8

Leo 'The Lion': signs, 14;
 personality, 37, 39; Lion
 symbol of, 37; Fire sign,
 41; Man, 39–40; Woman,
 40; Child, 40–41;
 Affinities, 41
Libra 'The Balance': signs,
 14; personality, 47, 49;
 Scales symbol of, 47; Air
 sign, 49; Man, 49–50;
 Woman, 50, 51; Child, 51;
 Affinities, 51
Lunar month: Babylonians
 predict length of, 8

Mars, 15; planetary ruler of
 Scorpio, 55
Mayans of Mexico: stone
 calendar of, 13
Mercury, 15; planetary ruler
 of Gemini, 27; planetary
 ruler of Virgo, 43
Mesopotamia: astrology in, 7
Moon, 7; on Babylonian
 sculpture, 8; visited by
 astronauts, 13, 15;
 planetary ruler of Cancer,
 31
Müller, Johann 'Regio-
 montanus', 12

Naburiannu (*c*. 500 BC), 8
Nectanebus (*b*. 385 BC);
 earliest extant personal
 horoscope, 9
Neptune, 15; part-ruler of
 Pisces, 77
Nostradamus, Michael
 (*b*. 1503), 12

Pisces 'The Fishes': signs,
 15; personality, 75–6; two
 fishes symbol of, 75;
 Water sign, 75; Man,
 76–7; Boman, 77–8; Child,
 78–9; Affinities, 79
Plato: *The Timaeus*, 6; 7, 9,
 10
Pluto, 15
Ptolemy, Claudius, 9;
 Tetrabiblos, 9

Rome, astrology in, 10
Rulership, 15

Sagittarius 'The Archer': on
 Babylonian boundary
 stone, 8; signs, 14;
 personality, 57, 59; dual
 sign, 57; Fire sign, 62;
 Man, 59–61; Woman, 61;
 Child, 61–2; Affinities, 62
Saturn, 15; planetary ruler
 of Capricorn, 63; 'hard
 task-master', 63
Science: attitude to
 astrology, 13
Scorpio 'The Scorpion': on
 Babylonian boundary
 stone, 8; signs, 14;
 personality, 53–4; Eagle
 and Scorpion symbols of,
 53; 'fixed' Water sign, 53;
 Man, 54–5; Woman, 55–6;
 Child, 56; Affinities, 56
Star of Bethlehem, 10
Stars: used by primitive man
 as calendar and compass, 6
Stonehenge: astronomical
 observatory, 6
Sumerians, 7
Sun, 7; on Babylonian
 sculpture, 8; 15; planetary
 ruler of Leo, 37

Taurus 'The Bull': signs, 14;
 personality, 21, 23; Bull
 symbol of, 21; 'fixed'
 Earth sign, 21; Man, 23;
 Woman, 23–4; Child, 24–5;
 Affinities, 25
Tower of Babel (Babylon):
 step pyramid, 8

Uranus, 15; part-ruler of
 Aquarius, 69

Vernal equinox: start of
 Babylonian year, 8; 14
Virgo 'The Virgin': signs, 14;
 personality, 43–4; Virgin
 symbol of, 43; Earth sign,
 43; Man, 44–5; Woman,
 45; Child, 46; Affinities, 46

Watersigns: Cancer, 31–6;
 Scorpio, 53–6; Pisces, 75–9

Zodiac signs: selected by
 Babylonians, 8

The publishers thank the following for permission to reproduce photographs:
Trustees of the British Museum, 9 (*left*); 10 (*above*)
Department of the Environment, Copyright reserved to HM The Queen, 6
Musée National du Louvre, Paris: Photo René Percheron, 9 (*right*); Photo Photographie Giraudon, Paris, 11
Foto Biblioteca Vaticana, 10 (*below*)
Museum of the History of Science, Oxford, 13 (*right*)
Musée Bayeux: Photo Hamlyn Group Picture Library, 12
Photographie Giraudon, Paris, 13 (*left*)